TOWER

Bill Henderson is the author of *The Kid That Could*, a novel, and two memoirs, *His Son* and *Her Father*. He is the publisher and founder of Pushcart Press and the editor of the acclaimed Pushcart Prize series. He lives on Long Island and in Maine.

ALSO BY BILL HENDERSON

His Son
Her Father
The Kid That Could

T
O
W
E
R

FAITH, VERTIGO, AND AMATEUR CONSTRUCTION

BILL HENDERSON

NORTH POINT PRESS
A DIVISION OF FARRAR, STRAUS AND GIROUX / NEW YORK

North Point Press
A division of Farrar, Straus and Giroux
19 Union Square West, New York 10003

Distributed in Canada by Douglas & McIntyre Ltd.
Printed in the United States of America
Designed by Jonathan D. Lippincott
Published in 2000 by Farrar, Straus and Giroux
First North Point Press paperback edition, 2001

Library of Congress Cataloging-in-Publication Data
Henderson, Bill, 1941–
    Tower: faith, vertigo, and amateur construction / Bill Henderson.
        p.   cm.
    ISBN 0-86547-614-4 (pbk.)
    1. Towers—Design and construction—Popular works.   I. Title.
TA660.T6.H46 2000
690'.15—dc21   99-46384

The author gratefully acknowledges the following sources:

E. B. White, *Letters of E. B. White*, collected and edited by Dorothy Lobrano Guth. Copyright © 1976 by E. B. White. Reprinted with permission of HarperCollins Publishers.

James Joyce, *Ulysses*. Copyright © Estate of James Joyce. Reproduced with the permission of the Estate of James Joyce.

Carol Shields, *The Stone Diaries*. Copyright © 1993 by Carol Shields. Used by permission of Viking Penguin, a division of Penguin Putnam Inc.

Reynolds Price, *A Whole New Life*. Macmillan, 1994. Copyright © 1994 by Reynolds Price. Reprinted by permission of The Gale Group, www.galegroup.com.

W. B. Yeats, *The Collected Works of W. B. Yeats, Volume I: The Poems*, revised and edited by Richard J. Finneran. Copyright © 1924 by Macmillan Publishing Company, renewed 1952 by Bertha Georgie Yeats. Reprinted with the permission of Simon and Schuster.

The Poems of W. B. Yeats: A New Edition, edited by Richard J. Finneran. Copyright 1933 by Macmillan Publishing Company; copyright renewed © 1961 by Bertha Georgie Yeats. Reprinted with the permission of Simon and Schuster.

A Vision. Copyright 1937 by W. B. Yeats; copyright renewed © 1965 by Bertha Georgie Yeats. Reprinted with the permission of Scribner, a division of Simon and Schuster.

John Cole, *In Maine*. Copyright © 1974 by John Cole. Used by permission of Penguin Putnam Inc.

for Deborah Morrison Henderson

TOWER

TOWER?

A few summers ago in Maine, I built a tower on a high hill overlooking the sea. This is a book, both practical and personal, about why and how I raised that tower.

If you have ever considered constructing a tower in your backyard—or if you have ever suffered from vertigo or a wavering of your faith—you may be interested in this little volume.

Tower in summer [*Bill Henderson*]

You may think that building a tower is beyond your reach, that it has to be a huge swaying beast, like Chicago's Sears Tower or one of the towers of New York's World Trade Center. But in my case, three stories, counting the deck at the peak, suited me just fine.

You may wish to go higher, and I suggest that you go as high as you like, but in many communities zoning restrictions will hold you below the treetops. You are, after all, contemplating an impractical, frivolous, and idiosyncratic structure, and zoning rules are designed to protect real estate values against the likes of you. A tower down the road is not what most citizens fancy. Also, your next-door neighbor may worry that you will block the sun (try not to).

And of course, as I did, you will have to endure the ever-ready phallus-substitute cracks. When this happens, point out to your detractors that the poet William Butler Yeats also had to listen to similar Freudian cheap shots from his friend Ezra Pound, who ignorantly dubbed Yeats's Thoor Ballylee "Ballyphallus." You might tell your critics that the historical connection of sex and towers has more to do with the Babylonian god Marduk frolicking with a priestess atop his giant ziggurat than any mere physical resemblance of organ and object.

Failing this, you might avoid the word "tower" and tell naysayers, your zoning board, and neighbors that you are planning a studio, a slim, tall studio. "Studio" carries a tone of seriousness, culture, and the rest. People like that.

If you live in the country, as I do part of the year, you may build any tower you like without too many explanations. I include several tower appreciations later that you may want to contemplate in planning your own spire.

I prefer a tower that stands by itself, unattached to house or other structure, and that is not built for practical, religious, or propagandist purposes. This preference leaves out a host of things that would like to call themselves towers, like the Canadian National Railroad Tower in Toronto (1,805 feet) and the wire-supported towers in Fargo, North Dakota (2,063 feet), and Warsaw, Poland (2,117 feet).

I do not appreciate phony towers like Howard Roark's titanic fictional skyscraper in Ayn Rand's novel *The Fountainhead* or Donald Trump's nonfiction fake, Trump Tower. These I classify as mere utilitarian erections. They are named towers for the romance of the term, but there isn't a rivet of romance in them.

Like all skyscrapers, they were conceived thanks to the fateful invention of the Otis elevator in 1857.

Mr. Otis made the climbing of stairs unnecessary. It was only a matter of time before the first skyscraper appeared, in 1883, and the race upward was on. Soon a slew of faux towers shot up, each aiming to be loftier and more imposing than somebody else's peak, and always symbolizing the overpowering interest of financial returns in a frenzied commercial culture that cares for little else. These air-conditioned beehives are all business: not an ounce of fun or folly in any of them.

Other towers you will not find in these pages: fire towers, transmission towers, gun towers (with one exception), grain silos, Muslim prayer towers, church steeples, the Washington Monument, grain elevators, tuna boat towers, water towers, the Statue of Liberty, gas towers, lighthouses—anything that has been thrust up with some practical, religious, or propagandist agenda.

About "thrust up": this book's towers reach to the sky; they do not thrust; although some, like the Tower of Babel, do a bit of thrusting and reaching at the same time, and there's a tad of propaganda in Babel, too. No tower is perfect, including my own, as will become quickly apparent.

Before I leave the bogus phallic symbolism issue entirely, I might note that the preferred angle of an alert penis is 45 degrees downward in most cases and almost never straight up like a tower. And in tower building, size does not matter. In fact, small is lovely. Consider, for instance, Winifred Lutz's art installation in Abington, Pennsylvania—a roofless stone tower that she aligned perfectly to capture the sun's rays through narrow slits at the winter solstice. Her delightful whimsy is only fifteen feet tall.

Stokes Castle in Nevada's Shoshone Mountains is a square three-story plaything built for the mining and railroad baron Anson Phelps Stokes in 1896. Situated just off the Pony Express Trail at 6,431 feet elevation, Stokes's tower is modeled on ancient buildings he had admired while touring Rome. Stokes occupied it for two months in the summer of 1897 and then abandoned it forever. You can visit Stokes Castle near Austin, Nevada, and marvel at the fresh, clean air, the enormous views, and the silence of the Shoshones. Perhaps it was the silence that scared off the busy Stokes.

Less lonely but even smaller is the sixteen-square-foot Teahouse Tower on Fanette Island in California's Lake Tahoe. Constructed of rough stones in 1929, it is sited on a hill and is almost as wide as it is high. The island and its tower are a child's fantasyland.

There are hundreds, if not thousands, of tiny towers to appreciate. You remember how as a child you made them out of sand or blocks or tin cans? Such a memory inspired the psychiatrist Carl Gustav Jung to raise his own tower on the banks of a Swiss lake. Two inches or 3,000 feet, the size of the tower is of no importance. All are mere pebbles on the earth's surface. It is the tall imagination that counts, in this book at least.

And the utter joy of building counts, too. As I said, my tower on that Maine hill is only three stories high, including the roof deck. Building up to that deck— with simple tools, no electricity, and little help—was a major satisfaction, indeed a salvation, during a year that saw several of my young friends diagnosed with cancer, my marriage shaken, and my faith often in shambles.

As E. B. White, the *New Yorker* writer, who once lived near my hill in the village of Brooklin, said: "Practically the most satisfying thing on earth (especially after fifteen years of trying to put English sentences together against time) is to be able to square off a board of dry white pine, saw to the line (allowing for the thickness of the pencil point) and have the thing fit perfectly."

Practically nothing in my tower fit perfectly, but I tried to make it fit well enough so that the tower would not topple in the first gust.

Winifred Lutz's tower [*Gregory Benson*]

Since there are no books or plans for building towers, if I had questions I visited people who were house-, shed-, or barn-building in the area and studied how they framed, sheathed, and roofed.

Or I talked to my friend A. J. Billings, proprietor of Barter's Lumber in Deer Isle. A.J. knows his sticks, and he's a superb teacher. He's a first-rate trumpeter, too, the star of the island's Fourth of July ceremonies. During the parade, A.J. and the dozen members of the town band sit on folding chairs on a slight rise in a field at the end of Deer Isle village's tiny main street. Everybody shows up for the parade and many of the residents concoct homemade floats and polish up old cars to participate. A.J. and the band vigorously play "Semper Fidelis," "The Thunderer," "The Stars and Stripes Forever," and all the marches by Maine composer R. B. Hall in their repertoire, which is considerable. Every summer, A.J. flies to New York City for bugle lessons.

A.J. taught me all I know about building, and he was ready with his Maine humor, too, comparing me to Tom Sawyer in the woods and joking about my tower blowing down with me on it. In Maine you know you have been provisionally accepted in the construction fraternity when you're the butt of jokes like that.

LOT

I built my tower near Sedgwick, Maine, a village not on most maps. Sedgwick is at the southern tip of a peninsula that extends into the Atlantic Ocean, bordered on the west by the Penobscot River, which drains much of upstate Maine, and on the east by Blue Hill Bay.

Once you have traveled on consumer-devoured and consumer-devouring U.S. Route 1 and turned onto that peninsula, you are in a different country. You will know you have arrived there because people wave to each other and to strangers as they pass. E. B. White described returning to this area as "the sensation of having received a gift from a true love."

Sedgwick village is about eight miles from White's farm in Brooklin. You reach Sedgwick from Brooklin by crossing the Benjamin River—more of a long tidal inlet than a proper river—on a rock causeway. The river joins Eggemoggin Reach at Sedgwick Harbor, home to about thirty working and pleasure boats.

There's a simple pontoon dock on that small harbor and in the summertime kids fish from the dock and swim in the water, which rarely gets over 55 degrees, except for maybe two weeks at the end of August.

The sun washes the land and water of this whole peninsula with a pale yellow light and the sky is constantly and brilliantly changing like a slow-motion kaleidoscope.

Sedgwick village has a country store, a post office, a library that opens a few hours a week, and a half-dozen houses at the river bend that are painted the very un-Maine colors of chartreuse, mauve, and tan. There's an old folks' home of clustered bungalows and a gold-domed Baptist church, and a carpenter's shop in a garage attached to the carpenter's house, plus a small antique and knickknack shop at the home of a lady who sells "fine handknit sweaters" which she makes right there.

Sedgwick village is this sort of place: At about six one morning I stopped in at the general store to buy a fresh blueberry muffin and coffee from Gretchen, the owner. I sat on the hood of my car near the causeway as the sun rose behind me and a woman and a young boy led a procession over the river: four huge, clomping workhorses and a happy mongrel dog—on their way to a field for the horses' breakfast, I guessed.

"Hi!" called the woman to the stranger sitting on his car hood eating a muffin in the early light.

"Good morning!" I waved, moved by her simple greeting. In my home "away" from Maine, we see no such processions, and strangers on car hoods at 6 a.m. are regarded with suspicion.

Not many tourists pass through Sedgwick village. Most of them take the turnoff at Route 15 a few miles to the west on the trip to or from Blue Hill, Ellsworth, and Route 1. It's more of a direct line and saves them five minutes. For what? I don't know. The slow and steady pace of the woman, the boy, the horses, and the mutt is not valued in the age of E-mail.

Because of this pace, many residents of this peninsula live decades longer than people from "away," despite a climate that can be brutal, especially in the winter. As the Maine poet Edwin Arlington Robinson wrote, "Maine is where children learn to walk on frozen toes."

E. B. White endured over fifty winters here. In a letter dated February 13, 1972, he wrote from his Brooklin saltwater farm: "About ten days ago we had a tremendous gale. Our power was gone most of the night, trees went down, and the Deer Isle Bridge pulled a tendon. It's a lofty bridge, and when it gets slatting around in a high wind it seems to lose its cool."

The terrific winter winds may be why Down East Maine is not known for its towers. Hardly a winter passes without a major nor'easter with near-hurricane-force winds. Some of these storms are still talked about in Sedgwick, particularly the 1898 "Portland Gale" that struck just after Thanksgiving and sank the 291-foot side-wheeler *Portland* with the loss of 171 passengers and crew. On land 456 people were killed up and down the coast in winds that reached 72 miles an hour.

Down East Maine's worst snowstorm hit on December 30–31, 1962. That storm looped out to Nova Scotia and then perversely swung back counterclockwise to the west and dumped over forty inches of snow in the Sedgwick area, creating drifts up to twenty feet and temperatures that dropped to fifteen degrees below zero in fifty-mile-an-hour winds.

Still to come was the great ice storm of January 8, 1998, which flattened huge electric transmission erections. *The New York Times* described it as "a Robert Frost nightmare of birches cracked in two by their own glazed weight, of proud Down Easters forced from their heatless homes, of nearly half a million people without power for days . . . 'The biggest disaster ever to hit this state,' said Angus King, Maine's Governor."

Clearly, on this coast, one builds with care.

But I had been summering here for many years and had recently constructed a cottage on Deer Isle, across the Eggemoggin Reach from Sedgwick. Before that cottage, I had never built anything much. I made up the cottage as I went along, with good advice from A.J. at the lumberyard. My tools were a hammer, a handsaw, a Tri-Square, a tape measure, a level, and a 25-foot length of ¼-inch Manila rope. I did most of the labor myself, except for the laying of the cement slab and the shingling of the roof (by the time I got to the roof my hands were dead and could hammer no more). I lost twenty unwanted pounds and, except for my numb hands, became strong again.

That cottage was finished now, a sad time really. My great joy had been in the making of it, an obsession perhaps. This was, after all, *home*. And I had made home there on the island. A summer home for my little family.

I had never heard of Christy Hill until February 1995, when a local real estate agent, aware of my interest in land with a water view, and with sympathy for my limited bank account, mailed me a grainy photocopy of a small lot with distant views of the ocean glittering like a thin string of light on the horizon. Not very promising, I thought, but I needed the drive to Maine and the infusion of energy that I always get from the stupendously beautiful Down East coast.

I had just finished writing about my daughter's birth eleven years before and about how Holly, in her growing up, taught her dad all he had once known but had forgotten (and would forget again).

Her Father is also the story of my wife, Annie, and me. It's about our first meeting at a New York literary cocktail party, where among other drunken achievements I hugged Walter Cronkite, insulted Norman Mailer, and kissed the sister of the President of the United States, evangelist Ruth Carter Stapleton, on the lips and then launched into a boozy rendition of the hymn "Trust and Obey" ("Trust and obey for there's no other way to be happy in Jesus but to trust and obey"). I did not know these people and would not know them in the future. I did not remember meeting Annie, until she tracked me down weeks later at my Bleecker Street apartment.

I was at the time a "wretch" like the one in the hymn "Amazing Grace." I was "blind" and I had not yet begun to "see" again. That Annie and I eventually married after a long, impossible affair; that in middle age we had a glorious child, Holly, conceived against all medical odds; that we continued to cling to and often adore each other—all of this was indeed evidence of grace. And much of that grace shines through Holly, I wrote.

Her Father is also Annie's tale. The daughter of often alcoholic parents from Holly Springs, Mississippi, Annie hit New York City in the mid-sixties intending to become an actress, but instead stumbled into a business she founded with a friend, Super Girls ("we do anything legal"). Mostly what Annie did legal was to stage fancy parties and run wacky errands for celebrity sorts.

Annie had offices in three cities and dozens of employees—Danielle Steel, now the pop scrivener, was one. Annie herself became celebrated—as a guest on *The Johnny Carson Show*, in a three-page *Look* magazine feature, and as co-host of her own daytime TV talk show.

At age twenty-five, through her beauty, her wit, and her wonderful, whole-hearted laugh, Annie owned New York for a nanosecond. But when I met her a decade later she was living out of a suitcase in sublet rooms, having just split up with her actor boyfriend. She had long been contracted to write a book about bananas for the American Banana Institute, but she hadn't written word one.

Her Father is also a memoir about my mother and the promise I made to her as she lay dying of cancer in the hospital. I said I would marry Annie and have the grandchild she always wanted. Mom had lived long enough to see all her three children grow up (I was almost forty when she died) and to hear of my New York bachelor romps after my first wife, an ex-nun, left me. I baffled my mother.

Her death was like her life, trusting, unafraid, never complaining, anticipating her journey to heaven where she would for sure find my long-dead father. She had been a deacon in the Presbyterian church, a popular math teacher at the local high school, where she also coached the cheerleaders, and a volunteer for Meals on Wheels and other good people. Just as important, I note in the memoir, she was the steadying force behind her God-obsessed, shy, and often silent husband, Francis, a man who trusted Jesus to heal all ills and would have condemned his children to the same faith healing had not our more practical mom intervened and taken us off to dentists and doctors.

After years of being written, more being rewritten (every comma had to be correct, every memory exact), and many rejections, twenty-seven of them, my memoir about the three women in my life had finally been accepted by a publisher in Boston. I drove there, delivered the manuscript to my editor, Betsey Uhrig, at Faber and Faber, and headed north to Maine with my beagle, Opie, and the balance of Faber's modest advance check in my pocket. I needed to see Maine again. I was emptied out. And my daughter was no longer a child: our baby didn't need her dad as much anymore. Memoir finished, baby gone, I felt hollow inside. Restless. Perhaps more depressed than I realized.

The real estate agent gave me general directions to Christy Hill. I asked for help at the Sedgwick general store and was told to circle the Baptist church and head straight up. Since the hill is almost 400 feet high, I expected a dramatic rise from sea level, but my ascent was a gradual one of soft inclines and plateaus through a mixed forest of spruce and maple, beech and birch.

Halfway up, I asked a lady walking her dog, "Where's Christy Hill?"

"You're on it," she informed me.

Up I drove for another mile until the road peaked in an expanse of blueberry fields. It rounded a bend, changed to dirt, and headed north. Hearing my rackety car, three deer bounded across the white fields. The sun's glare off the snow made it hard to see, but finally I spotted the broker's sign that marked the lot, swinging on its hinges in the wilderness.

I stopped the car and Opie and I got out to look around. To the northeast, in the clear cold air, was the crown of Blue Hill, lofting over Blue Hill village at its base, scene of the annual Blue Hill Fair, the inspiration for E. B. White's tale of Wilbur the pig and Charlotte the spider. Twenty miles to the east across Blue Hill Bay were the mountains of Acadia National Park's Mt. Desert Island, and below me were Swans Island and dozens of lesser islands and ledges, fringed with ice. Beyond them the open ocean stirred quietly.

I walked through the woods 160 feet to the stone wall at the rear of the lot, where I discovered more acres of blueberry fields and, miles away, light fog rising off the Penobscot River and, still farther in the distance, the mountains of the northwest. I imagined I could just make out the top of Mt. Katahdin in Baxter State Park, Maine's highest peak, or was it Mt. Washington in New Hampshire?

Opie took off after a scent, howling in the stillness. I sat on that old stone wall for a long time, stunned by this sacred place.

There was no way I could afford it, I thought. My advance would cover only a portion of the asking price. Besides, what was this really but a 1.78-acre subdivision in the middle of nowhere?

More important, how could I explain my infatuation to my wife? Annie might point out that we already had the summer cottage on Deer Isle that I had spent years building obsessively. No way did we need another lot in Maine, she'd say, perhaps rising to operatic hyperbole about my edifice complex. She might remind me that we often couldn't pay our bills, particularly that fuel bill last winter. The oil company had cut off deliveries, the furnace had quit, and we had endured a chilly week in our Long Island home until we'd scraped together enough cash to pay up. She would bring to my attention my dying Oldsmobile station wagon with over 160,000 miles on the odometer, held together with duct tape. And I'd have to admit that my publishing company, Pushcart Press, had been hanging on by its financial fingernails for twenty-three years and had frequently relied on a cash miracle or the kindness of friends to bail it out.

What would I do with this lot? I asked myself on that wall.

Well, if I bought it, maybe just leave it alone, I answered.

This was ridiculous. Buying it made no sense whatsoever. But at that time "sense" was not what I was about.

Opie beagled across the fields, howling insanely, chaotically chasing any scent he crossed, and ignoring my calls.

Because of such uncontrolled passions, Opie—son of Bruno the Duke of Eqununk and Lady Sand Pebbles III—had so exasperated his original owners a few years earlier that they were about to condemn him to the dog pound, when Holly and I rescued him. But Opie had never been a happy beagle on Long Island. He needed lots of smells and room to smell them in. Because of his super nose, Opie knew things I could never know, a universe of spirit and substance forever beyond my dim powers. In Maine he was in sniff heaven, his first blueberry fields. Grumpy Opie was on a rip.

I ran after him, finally caught him up in my arms, and carried him to the car. It was the only way to snap him out of his nose dreams.

NEGOTIATION

Opie and I sped down slippery Christy Hill to the phone booth outside the post office. I opened negotiations with the broker, a friend who had paced many blazed property lines with me over the years. Rich Lord is his name, an honest, smart young man, although selling real estate in the area had left him neither rich nor a lord. In fact, he lived in a trailer.

"Rich, that land is incredible! The mountains, the islands, the ocean. I can see Ireland!" I sang as I offered a price well below what the owner was asking.

Tip: Never wax rhapsodic about a property that you want to buy cheaply.

"I'll call the owner and get back to you," said Rich.

Opie and I hurried to the general store for a cup of coffee and returned to the post office to wait in the cold for the phone to ring. When it did, Rich's answer was brief. The owner demanded his price and nothing less.

I caved in immediately. "He's right! It's worth more than that!" I blurted.

Later, I learned that the owner had purchased this entire six-acre ridge only a few years earlier for a fraction of what I was paying.

No matter. Opie and I ecstatically hiked our lot until the sun set over the mountains and a hard, bitter northwest wind started to blow. That night the thermometer dropped to just above zero and the wind neared twenty knots. In the cottage, the furiously burning woodstove was little help. I burrowed down deep in my sleeping bag, guaranteed effective by L.L. Bean to zero, and pulled Opie on top of the bag, covering him with an old rug. In the morning, the plastic water jug was frozen solid.

I telephoned Annie on Long Island about my discovery. "No contract yet. I can still change my mind. Do you want to come up here and walk the land?" I asked.

"Maybe in warmer weather."

"It might be sold by then. I know you'll love it. I've been looking for this for years. It's the top of the world!"

"I'll come in the spring," she repeated. "You'd better think about it."

She had a point. In this cold I couldn't think clearly about anything else but trying to get warm.

It was Sunday morning. Anxious to talk about my lot, on impulse I telephoned my friend Doris Grumbach in the little town of Sargentville, just the other side of the Deer Isle bridge. Doris, an author and National Public Radio book critic, had recently moved here from Washington, D.C., with her friend Sybil Pike, proprietor of Wayward Books, a rare and out-of-print book business that had journeyed north with them to a shop by a quiet cove off Eggemoggin Reach.

"Can I drive you to church?" I asked Doris, and she said I could.

Doris is more than just a friend. A few years earlier at the Stonington Episcopal Church, Doris, a lay reader in the church, had served my entire family Communion. Holly was about six then, and I remember the tiny pocketbook at her feet when she knelt with Annie and me at the altar, and her straw hat and white gloves as she leaned forward to drink from the cloth-wrapped chalice that Doris offered her. "This is Christ's blood, shed for you," Doris told us, words that I had heard from various ministers at hundreds of Communions over the years, but never with such impact as now, spoken by a friend to my family. As we knelt there by the rail with many others, I thought I would cry out.

This frozen morning, I picked up Doris in the duct-taped car and made a place for her to sit with a coat over the remains of the front-seat upholstery that Opie had torn up for a nest the previous winter. We drove north to St. Francis-by-the-Sea, near Blue Hill. The church sits on a hill in the woods, having been relocated there after the congregation decided to saw it in half, truck it to the spot, and reassemble it, steeple and all. Moving big buildings is a Maine tradition. Not much is knocked down or thrown out here.

I remember that Sunday morning at St. Francis as wonderfully clear, with a light coating of fresh snow in the silent spruce forest around us. I didn't know it at the time, but this would be one of the last occasions that Doris would serve as a reader of the church. She was distancing herself from organized religion and would soon become a contemplative and write about the experience in her moving memoir *The Presence of Absence*. She was nearing eighty, the mother of four daughters and three times a grandmother. The years ahead would bring her illness and pain, but neither of us knew this on that spectacular Sunday.

After church, eager for her opinion of my discovery, I drove her to the top of Christy Hill and pointed out the distant views across the fields.

"What are you going to do here?" she asked.

"I don't know. Probably leave it as it is. It's perfect. No houses, no people, wild."

Doris, who is always careful with her words, said nothing.

In my mind suddenly was a vision of a stone tower on a moonlit cliff—right out of some forgotten nineteenth-century romantic English novel. I didn't tell Doris about my vision. She might have questioned my taste, if not my sanity. A nineteenth-century tower? What could that possibly mean?

"Maybe I'll build a tower here." I laughed and started the car.

Back at their house by the cove, Sybil waited with coffee and scones. Sybil, who is Jewish by birth, professes no particular faith and is sometimes skeptical of various enthusiasms.

I tried out my tower inspiration on her, again leaving out the details about the moonlit cliff.

"Why a tower?" she asked.

I shrugged. "I don't know. No reason. Why do I need a reason?"

Sybil raised an eyebrow at me over her scone. The three of us gazed quietly out at the ice-jammed cove.

"That's it. A tower for no reason," I said finally, breaking the silence.

MARDUK'S PILE

Sedgwick is a long way from East Hampton, New York, where I live most of the year with my family in the working-class section called Springs. Our neighbors are fishermen, mechanics, carpenters, and artists. Jackson Pollock's house, now a museum, is just down the street.

Unlike quiet Sedgwick, East Hampton, at the eastern end of Long Island, is easy to find, and notorious. During the warm months it is gridlocked with celebrity gods and goddesses and tourists seeking them—Hollywood East.

The town dump is the major tower in East Hampton. Many summer-home owners here are wealthy, often for doing rather little. They, and most other residents, allow themselves to be called "consumers"—like the biblical hordes of locusts that consumed entire harvests—and, true to the term, they buy stuff and throw it away quickly so they can consume more. That's how the dump grew.

Officially, they now call the dump a "transfer station." The piles of waste just climbed too high and the stuff now has to be hauled away, transferred to nobody knows where. But the transfer station also features a thriving "take it or leave it" exchange section for usable discards. I mined this section for the windows, doors, and furniture for my tower.

There is only one nonutilitarian tower in East Hampton town—Harold Wit's forty-footer near the beach. Built three decades ago, Wit's rising tower was protested by his neighbors at the time, who complained that he might want to peer into their backyards and upstairs windows. Wit, then a bachelor, explained to the building inspector that he would be having

Harold Wit's tower [Lily Henderson]

more fun inside his tower of a weekend than his neighbors and peeping on their recreations was of no interest. The inspector thought this a reasonable argument, and let Wit's whimsy rise.

Now building here, especially for amateurs like me, is no fun. The building inspector is paranoid about all new construction—there's so much of it—and he and his posse supervise the driving of each nail. There are codes on everything, height in particular, and rules that you need a Ph.D. in advanced mathematics and a team of crack lawyers to figure out.

But old spires of another sort abound—church steeples. To most of those who make offerings at the dump, these steeples mean little, but to me, the child of religious parents, they evoke a deep, if distant, passion.

As a boy in Philadelphia, I attended church with my mother, father, brother, and sister every Sunday morning and evening and again on Wednesday night for hymn-sing. We said prayers before every meal and read the Bible and recited Bible verses after dessert.

Pop insisted on our devotion.

He spent his entire adult life, almost four decades, traveling for the General Electric Company as an engineer in charge of repairing low-voltage industrial switch gear. While he traveled he prayed without ceasing. I described my father in a memoir, *His Son*, published quietly in 1981.

On his trips, Pop was addicted to the frightful radio bombast of evangelists Carl McIntire and Oral Roberts, who preached fire and damnation for communists and other nonbelievers and heavenly bliss for the likes of Pop and his family. In order to be sure I was safe from God's furnace, I missed not one Sunday for over a decade, starting in nursery school. I was awarded a gold bar for every one of those years. The string of bars was stuck right there on the lapel of my sports jacket: a perfect record, and one of the longest periods of Sunday school attendance in the recent history of the national Presbyterian church.

Pop was certain about eternal burnings for the unsaved dead, but he was incredibly tender to all living beings. He never struck me in anger, and the only time he accidentally smacked me, he fell into spasms of apology. He was so gentle that he refused to prune live limbs on trees in our backyard. During our annual one-day summer fishing trip on the Ocean City, New Jersey, bay, he wouldn't bait his hooks with live minnows. Instead, he brought along frozen clam strip bait and was quite happy to catch nothing at all. I gladly skewered the squirming minnows and hoped for a prize flounder.

Pop's idea of a cuss word was "heck," and "sex" was unmentionable. In order to marry my mother, he had to be persuaded by her that Luke 20:35—"They which shall be accounted worthy to obtain . . . the resurrection from the dead, neither marry, nor are given in marriage"—was overruled by Mark 10:6–8—"God made them male and female. For this cause shall a man leave his father and mother and cleave to his wife; and they twain shall be one flesh."

On dates, my father and mother knelt and asked God for directions in their courtship. I know all of this because after Pop's funeral—he died quietly in his sleep at age sixty-four, having said his bedside prayers—I raided my mother's trove of old letters, hunting for information about my silent father's life. In a letter dated May 26, 1938, as their wedding approached, he reminded her: "What really matters now is our relationship between God and ourselves."

I think Pop would have liked to become an evangelist, but he was too agonizingly shy. On one of the few scraps of paper he left behind from his college days, I found this resolve to himself: "Have fellowship with whomever you meet and witness the love of God which passes understanding . . . Be not ashamed of God in any sense for He is my life and in Him I have

my being." But when guests appeared at the door to
our house, Pop fled to his basement workshop and let
Mom handle the chin music.

When I was a kid, I was sure Pop had it right. While
the world burned around us in World War II and
Korea, our family waited together for the Rapture. I
remember the first appearance of a young new evangelist in Ocean City—Billy Graham. Pop and I went to
hear him at the boardwalk Music Pier one Saturday
evening in the summer of 1948. I was only seven, but
when Billy asked all those he had converted to born-
again status to come forward, I raised my hand and
trotted to the podium while Pop beamed at me and the
organ played softly "Just As I Am."

Afterward, Pop and I walked hand in hand down
the boardwalk and, just as Billy Graham promised, I
felt all my sins had been lifted from me (whatever
those sins were—picking my nose? swatting my
younger brother, Bob?). I had become so very light. I
could almost soar. Pop and I would save all of those
boardwalk strollers for Jesus. I was certain of it. In fact,
we'd save the entire world.

That winter I tried out my missionary skills in the
snow. After a sudden inspiration, I interrupted a sledding party on our suburban street and asked the kids to
form a circle on their sleds. I told them to bow their

heads in prayer and ask Jesus to save them. They did. But after that, I had nothing more to say, so we headed back to the sledding hill whooping and hollering as before.

But as I grew up, lusted in my heart after girls, and entertained thoughts of becoming President of the United States and other standard American passions, Pop's simple faith left too much unexplained. "If you don't know, I can't tell you," he'd say dismissively when I asked him why Jews, Hindus, and Muslims had to burn in hell. And he was fanatic about booze. When I was ten, he commanded me to sign a life-time family covenant promising never to use alcohol. I signed, but I had no idea what the stuff was or why he was so concerned. (It turned out his father, a horse-and-wagon meat-delivery man for Swift and Co., was a ghastly drunk when Pop was a boy.)

As for girls, no way was I attending the elementary school's sixth-grade dance instruction class, Pop said. Dancing was forbidden in the Bible, according to him. Mom had another idea of the Bible. She convinced him it would be okay if I learned the social graces and a fox-trot or box step. So off to dance lessons I went while Pop shook his head in disapproval.

Suddenly Pop's faith answered none of my questions. His "Be good" or "Be sure to marry a Christian

girl" just didn't cover it. His silence left me abandoned. I became fatherless and adrift.

I tried "reason" and proclaimed the "New Age of
Reason" in a high school newspaper editorial. Abolish
religions and ideologies, I demanded. As editor-in-
chief I pretty much ordered what I wished. A few
friends and I started a philosophy club, where on
Saturday nights we debated the ideas of Nietzsche and
Camus and the existence of God (I was still in God's
corner) and how to score with girls.

When that club led nowhere, I broke away
and announced the Thoreau Club. Only those kids
who recognized the "truth" would be welcome in
my new club, which would meet high in a tiny room
in the high school attic. But I never could come
up with words for what that "truth" was, and we never
had one meeting or inducted one member besides
myself.

For a decade I wandered, in college and afterward,
adopting the personality of one strong mentor after
another, often near despair and once at least passively
suicidal (I didn't care if a truck flattened me). But as I
hit bottom, I realized that Pop had left me his kindness, his caring, the possibility of something sacred.
Indeed, "Life is sacred" became the idea I clutched as
I was about to go under.

Because of Pop's stubborn, inchoate passion for Jesus, I survived. In a way, that Billy Graham evening in 1948 wasn't as silly as it sounds. I just had to learn time and time again what God's love means.

About towers I had thought not one iota for all those fatherless years, until that day with Doris on Christy Hill and my idea of a "tower for no reason."

Maybe memories of the Tower of Babel had sprung up from my biblical grab bag that day. "Go to, let us build us a city and a tower, whose top may reach unto heaven," reports Genesis on the plans for that tower.

The details of Babel's construction are left out of the narrative, but its fate is not. God didn't appreciate uninvited visitors. He cast Babel's builders from a one-language Eden into a babel of tongues so that "they may not understand one another's speech." Construction ended, the tower was obliterated.

In my flailing adolescence, I always imagined that Babel's tower was yet another fake meant to terrify kids like me about the consequences of thinking too highly of themselves. But Babel was no fake. A tower like

Tower of Babel in Construction, by Breughel [CORBIS/Francis G. Mayer]

Babel did exist—many of them did. They were called ziggurats, terraced pyramid-style heaps lofted to praise and often to house the god of the moment.

The earliest ziggurat, and perhaps the model for all that followed, may have been the Sumerian temple tower dedicated to the moon god Nanna at Ur. That tower, dating from 2100 B.C.E., was estimated to be only seventy feet tall. But, as we have noticed with contemporary skyscrapers, the urge to compete in reaching to the heavens was irresistible and higher ziggurats followed.

Word of these towers reached the writer of that Genesis passage and he spun a fine fiction, but the real giant, erected by Nebuchadnezzar II, wasn't completed until after Genesis was composed.

Construction started in 629 B.C.E. and lasted decades. It took a year just to make the bricks, 58 million of them. You can still find these bricks in modern Babylon, stamped with the royal imprint and used as a portion of a dam across the Euphrates River. The tower itself is just a watery hole in the ground.

But in its day, E-temen-anki, "House of the Foundation of Heaven and Earth," was one of the spectacles of the ancient world: a square eight-story structure, 298 feet on each side and about 300 feet tall, with a 100-foot entrance ramp and seven terraces that rose from its base to the residence of the god Marduk at the peak.

The god's room there was sparsely furnished—a table and a couch where the priestess "gave the god pleasure." Genesis is correct; a tower like this did pretend to "reach unto heaven." But Marduk, unlike the Hebrew God, didn't seem to mind a bit.

The historian Herodotus visited Babylon around 460 B.C.E. and apparently was allowed to visit Marduk's room. He reported: "There is no statue of any kind set up in the place, nor is the chamber occupied of night by anyone but a single native woman who, as the Chaldeans, the priests of this god, affirm, is chosen for himself by the deity out of all the women of the land."

Eventually, it wasn't the Hebrew God who destroyed Marduk's pleasure palace, at least not directly. Xerxes captured Babylon and is said to have leveled the tower, as conquerors often do, knocking down the blocks of the loser.

Others surmise that the sheer weight of the tower caused its collapse: the bottom bricks just gave out and crumbled. Or perhaps an earthquake did it in. In any case, the term "act of God" is inserted in our architectural contracts even today.

Was that the reason behind my "no reason" when I began to build on Christy Hill? Was I attempting to reach God? Would God care about my tower? I barely gave it a thought.

I do note for the record, however, that my hill is almost 400 feet above sea level, which beat Marduk's pile by 100 feet before I even started.

STUBBY STEEPLE

The little church down the highway from our house in East Hampton has a stubby steeple. It leans backward, as if about to topple on the congregation. In this small wood-framed sanctuary, no bigger than a country storefront, I rediscovered the faith of my father, and lost it again.

Annie took Holly to Sunday school at the little church after she heard a friend's tale: The friend had invited her teenage daughter to church for the first time and the daughter thought it was all hilarious. She actually laughed out loud during the service.

Annie appreciated tradition: to her, church was ceremonies, songs, pageantry, and Sunday outfits. She wanted Holly to know these traditions and not think they were comic. So she dressed her up and enrolled her in the Sunday school.

"Where's Mr. Henderson?" the Irish minister asked at the coffee hour. "That's a good Presbyterian name."

Annie reported his interest to me, but I was having none of his church. The idea of walking through a church door after decades of absence evoked astonishing dread. Perhaps I thought I'd meet my father there. I'd have to deal all over again with his shyness and silence. I had a hot contempt for church doctrines and all who believed such tales. How brain-dead they seemed! Miracles! The Son of God! The Resurrection! Had they ever once thought about any of it? How annoying—and horrifying—that they might welcome me back with their Christian grins.

On the night of February 25, 1990, our part of Long Island was entombed by a record blizzard. Not much moved on Sunday morning, and the town's plows managed to cut only a narrow lane down the highway.

My usual Sunday morning ritual was common: a bagel and coffee in bed with *The New York Times*. But outside I could see no *Times* delivered on the mounds of snow that were increasing by the minute.

"We're off to church!" Annie announced through the door to the bathroom, where I sat on the toilet contemplating a *Times*less morning.

"You can't drive all the way down there!" I yelled.

"Yes I can!" she called back, with classic Annie defiance.

In seconds I reasoned that I had to get hold of a *Times* to survive the morning in good habit and that I could also chauffeur Holly and Annie to church safely. I'd buy a *Times* at the store, read it there, and pick them up after services.

But why not go to church too? My faith had never entirely left me, recurring as sudden spasms of longing.

A Zen monk once admitted that he received several enlightenments while evacuating of a morning. Doing the same, I pondered why I was so afraid of church. Hadn't I once jumped naked into a pile of fornicating strangers at New York's public orgy, Plato's Retreat, and thought it seemed like a form of religious communion? I hadn't feared that. Why now this terror? Coward.

"I'm coming, too," I hollered to Annie.

I pulled up my pants, found a tie, and we spun off into the blizzard.

The windshield wipers were frozen down. I couldn't free them. I did manage to clear a spot on the windshield but the wet snow quickly covered it. So I drove like a train engineer with my head out the window, very slowly, wiping my eyes with a handkerchief Annie handed me.

With Holly and Annie, I walked through the church door into a mostly empty room. Sunday school was canceled. The organist was snowed in and only a dozen people who lived nearby had turned out. The minister with his Santa Claus white beard carried us in song without the organ. Simple, tentative voices we had. I heard quiet people trying to carry a tune about a Lord who they hoped would save them somehow from private pain, dread, sorrow, confusion. Together we sang about what we could never have talked about face-to-face without music.

During the service, I was singled out by the minister as the stranger in the group and, as was the custom, I was asked to explain who I was and how I came to be there. I stood next to Holly and Annie and said, "I attended a Philadelphia Presbyterian church a long time ago. Today I got here with my head out the car window because the windshield wipers were stuck, and I couldn't see the road ahead of me."

The people laughed.

The minister's sermon was about heaven. It was intelligent and big news to me. He said heaven is here and now. Hell was never mentioned. This wasn't the story my father taught me. In my long exile from church, I never expected to hear words like this from the pulpit. No damnation? Only love?

On the following Sundays I came back for more of his words and I started to reconsider what I had rejected. My objections remained, but so what? Maybe this Jesus *was* just a local Jewish prophet. Maybe Paul tacked together the religion out of his own visions and used Jesus for his personal fantasies. Maybe Jesus never even existed. So what? "The myth contains the truth, not our own reasons," said C. S. Lewis. This Christianity was our myth, I now figured. We built this cathedral together over the centuries. The few dozen people in that little church helped build it every Sunday. And yes, people like us tore it down again and again in crusades, inquisitions, religious wars, lies, hatred; in short, in the sins we confessed to constantly. And then we reconstructed that church again. We sought God again.

And that God *is* love, the love these people sang to each other about in that small building, and the love that the new minister reminded us about in his Sunday tales.

At the center of all this was, of course, the figure of Jesus, a sweet, simple man betrayed by his disciples who said he was returning to take revenge on a nonbelieving world that had crucified him. As I saw it, our little church did not worship the blasphemy of Jesus the Avenger. Our Jesus was unconditional love, as the minister said.

He quoted Dietrich Bonhoeffer and Herman Melville and a host of poets. Harvey Cox, the Harvard divinity school professor, was a good friend. The minister said he had marched with Martin Luther King, Jr., in Selma. On King's birthday many of us went to the black church down the road and members of the two congregations celebrated King's life together.

The new minister's religion made the world seem wondrous again; it opened up and did not shut down the spirit. I learned, as if for the first time, the definitions of grace, reverence, and forgiveness.

Ceremonies that had been boring to me as a boy now became the focus of all meaning. Baptism, for instance. When Tyler Galloway, a member of the fourteenth generation of a family that had lived here since before the Revolutionary War, was baptized, the church spilled over with relatives and neighbors. At this ancient ritual in this timeless spot by the bay, we were all linked—to the past, to each other, and to the God of love, hidden from me for years.

I felt like a character out of a Flannery O'Connor story, relentlessly pursued by a God who had finally tracked me down in a snowstorm. "These stories are the heart of our civilization! They are who I am!" I declared in my journal.

To the amazement and chagrin of my friends, who considered religion to be a bizarre crock of superstition and hypocrisy, I rejoined the Presbyterians and reaccepted Christ as "my personal savior." I was member number 99 in the Napeague Church.

The minister became my friend and I his confidant. "I love you, Billy," he said. "You are very dear to me." And he meant it. He was the first man I had ever met who could use the word "love" to another man. We talked almost every day. I dubbed him the Bishop of Blarney because of his joy in a good story. He relished jokes—many of them about the Bible and its contradictions—and, as he grew more comfortable in his new church, he enjoyed a good gossip with me about members of his flock.

The "Bishop" thought he had come home. He hugged everybody. Hugged and hugged. He imagined that he was surrounded by the love he preached.

He was wrong.

Many in the church didn't appreciate his hugs. They wanted salvation, not squeezes. Bonhoeffer, Melville, the poets, and a Harvard professor were not who they expected to hear from on Sunday morning. These were hardworking people living from paycheck to paycheck. They sought certainties, not fancy words. If you wanted culture you should go south of the highway near the ocean beach and the big stone churches of the fancy set. The Bible recited as fact was what they were paying the minister for. And what was so funny? This wasn't an Irish party! Salvation was serious business.

The rumors began: the reverend was sleeping with women in the flock; he had slashed the tires of a session member; he had done things so horrible that the secrets could never be revealed to the general congregation. Anonymous hate letters about him turned up in our mailbox.

But many in the congregation supported the minister. He had injected life into the sleepy church and introduced many new members. This faction suggested raising his salary to a total of $22,000, in addition to his free house. The minister was miffed. He thought he deserved a bigger raise. When I suggested to him that serving God was salary enough, that he should work for nothing, he looked at me, uncomprehending.

There were catfights at session meetings, heavy-duty cusswords. In a tight vote, the session voted to take away the minister's key to the sanctuary. (He broke in, using a letter opener to spring the lock.) Half of the little congregation shunned the other half. One member said he'd flatten the minister if he ever tried to hug him again. The Long Island Presbyterian authorities were alerted to imminent civil war and the possibility of real violence.

The minister was lonely in the church of love, besieged, jumpy, and starting to lose it. To cheer him up I invited him to a book party at George Plimpton's house in New York. While there, he borrowed a book, slipping it into his coat pocket. Weeks later, he confessed all to George and begged forgiveness. "Why, Vicar, don't be upset. Everybody lifts my books," said George.

More disturbing to me was the Mother's Day caper. In need of flowers for his wife, the minister called a funeral director and asked for the location of a recent burial. He told me he was thinking of lifting a few stalks from the grave to present to his wife. "They would just wilt there," he explained to me. "Why spend fifty bucks?"

I worried about my friend. Why was Jesus of little comfort to him? "You are my mentor, Billy," he said. But I felt helpless.

His wife, too, was of little comfort to him. Her true god was spontaneity. She talked nonstop, chain-smoked, and tossed out words like "fuck" at church functions. Often she sang too loudly in the six-person, off-key choir, dominating it with her trained and lovely soprano voice. She was a talented cook and threw lavish parties in the church manse, where, after the minister gave the blessing, the name of Jesus seldom arose and booze was the dominant spirit.

An aspiring novelist and former English major, she announced plans to write a novel based on the minister's romantic involvements—something about Jane Fonda and others during his long preaching stint out West. She cleaned out the basement of the manse, set up an office and typewriter there, and promised to blow the whistle on the sex habits of the clergy in an explosive best-seller.

Prozac didn't seem to calm her much. After a few drinks, she hinted darkly about "killing the pastor." Just a metaphor, I hoped.

When she left East Hampton for a long stay with friends in England, the minister took up with a divorcing woman in the congregation. Some of his enemies lurked in the bushes of her house with a video camera. One night they got what they wanted: a clear shot of the minister in his bathrobe.

The Presbyterian authorities were informed of the tape and they canned the Bishop of Blarney forthwith. He was forbidden to ever enter the little church again. Crude crayoned images of him, with horns on his head, were tacked up in the Sunday school room where my daughter was taught. "Devil" was scrawled on them.

It was time for me and my family to leave the church. I was a two-time loser at organized religion. Holly said she was bored there anyway; Annie thought they were a nasty bunch.

I worried that my friend the minister would harm himself. The man who had showed me love in the church couldn't find it for himself.

Once again I spent Sunday mornings at home, paging through *The New York Times* with the rest of mercantile America. I couldn't explain to myself then, and still can't, why religion often kills the source that inspires it and doesn't seem to notice the slaughter. Perhaps the believers had heard words like "grace," "reverence," and "forgiveness" for so long that they were numb to their meanings.

To me, the stubby-steepled church now seemed to be just a contentious country club for people who couldn't get themselves invited to any other club.

But still, whenever I found myself in a church somewhere—as with Doris that morning in Blue

Hill—I could be ambushed by choking tears. I dealt with this in two ways. I sat near the door so I could vanish if I spun out of control. And, in my mind, I imagined myself hollering out loud to the people in the pews around me: "It's true! It's all true! Don't you see!"

LOVE IS GOD

Eight miles to the east from the peak of Christy Hill is the pointy steeple of the Brooklin Baptist Church. It is visible from the hill on all but the foggiest days. Thirty miles to the west, on the banks of the Penobscot River, is the sharp white steeple of the Stockton Springs Congregational Church. And just at the base of Christy Hill is the gold dome of the Sedgwick Baptist Church, a stranger in this country of white-needled spires.

I have never been inside any of these churches. Except for my visit to the Blue Hill church with Doris that winter morning, I had managed to ignore the calling of Sunday bells. What a racket, I thought.

These days I worshiped at the church of my daughter. When Holly was very young I tried to tell her about the Jesus I heard about when I was her age, but then she reversed the message and began to teach me.

I tried to explain Christmas to her. "It's a birthday party for a man named Jesus who lived long ago and said we should all love each other," I said, choking.

Concerned by my sadness, and hoping to cheer up me and Jesus, Holly said, "We could get him a Mr. Potato Head for his birthday."

While Holly learned about words like "Jesus" and "Christmas" from me, I relearned words like "wonder" and "love" from her. And, more important, I learned how not to be embarrassed by simple sentiments.

Wonder.

One morning Holly woke me quite early. "Daddy, come quick! It's 'mazing!"

She led her grumpy dad to her bedroom.

"See!" She pointed. A huge full moon was setting in the west and through another window the sun, even larger, was rising from the east at the same moment.

I sat with her on her bed and shared her awe.

Now and then I would stare at Holly in wonder. Her gentle face, her grace. Obviously God was a woman.

Then I would wonder at my wonder. Why didn't I spend every moment in amazement at her—at everybody? How could the life of a child, any life, become ordinary? Another drive to school, another trip to the grocery store, another book proposal to read, another evening meal? How could I allow any second to be routine?

To Holly no day was ordinary. Every moment was "'mazing."

Love.

With Holly no love was ever undemonstrated. Her good-night "I love you, Mommy, I love you, Daddy, I love you, Opie" was followed with hugs and kisses for all, especially the dog.

After our good nights, I'd sit next to her bed as she drifted off to sleep. I didn't want her to leave.

"You're a great kid, kid," I said.

"You're a great dad, Dad," she murmured, curling up.

Please don't sleep, Holly, I whispered to myself. Don't go to that other place. Stay a few minutes more.

To Holly love was as real as a rock. Her love was offered to her parents and friends without adult reservations, qualifications, or criticisms.

Once, I had forgotten to bring her lunch with us when I dropped her off at kindergarten with our usual good-bye hugs and kisses. I went home, retrieved the Big Bird lunch box, and reappeared at her school.

"Holly, look who's here!" called her teacher.

"Daddy!" Holly screamed, scrambling off the swing and rushing at breakneck speed across the school yard to crash into my arms.

"We forgot your lunch, Holly," I managed to say.

"I love my daddy."

I could only nod and hold Holly in her never-ending hug.

For Holly and her friends, affection was never muted. They didn't need a boozy cocktail party or a church moment of "peace" to inspire a kiss. Love was not just a word trotted out in a Sunday sermon and forgotten before the offering was taken. Their love for each other was a matter of every moment. To walk down the street holding hands or with their arms around each other wasn't a bit remarkable to them. Love was just the way it all was, from the center of the earth to the stars above.

From Holly I learned, as if for the first time, the meaning of Mark 10:15: "Whosoever shall not receive the Kingdom of God as a little child, he shall not enter therein."

Because of Holly I could appreciate Tolstoy's "Confession"—"I believe in a God who is for me spirit, love, the principle of all things . . . I believe that the reason of life is for each of us simply to grow in love."

From Holly's instruction, I now could figure out what Meister Eckehart meant when he said, "If you love yourself you love everybody else as you do yourself. As long as you love another person less than you love yourself, you will not really succeed in loving yourself."

Of course, all this was a matter of faith—the faith that life is worth loving. That faith is "the force of life," as Tolstoy said.

I paid no attention to the distant steeples as I wandered Christy Hill with my howling beagle that winter. It's all so simple and obvious, I thought. And it's not taught in church. People are complicated. God is simple. Love is God. And that God is so easy to know.

To remind myself of my new faith, I composed and tacked up my Holly creed to my cottage wall. "Bottom Line" it was headed.

> Our choice is love or despair. The argument for love? There is no argument for love. Love is nonrational, defiant faith. Love is constant caring, reverence, and wonder at each tremendous second.

Despair's argument? It's rational and submissive. We are born of a chance encounter of sperm and egg. We struggle to grow and reproduce and then we die. Our star will one day incinerate our earth and all evidence of us. Despair is boredom, carelessness, depression, madness.

There is only one sin and that is the failure to love.

Since we all constantly fail to love, we forgive ourselves and others always.

Love is God. The kingdom of that God is within you and all persons, always.

As a P.S. to whip-smart theologians who are baffled by the presence of evil in a God-created earth, I added: "Love does not cause earthquakes, famines, or holocausts."

And such a God does not knock down towers in Babylon, or Sedgwick.

VERTIGO

Since I couldn't dig my foundation on Christy Hill until the April thaw, I had the rest of the winter to dream my "tower for no reason."

I dreamed many towers, a jumble of spires, but still I couldn't forget that original and persistent epiphany with Doris on Christy Hill, an illustration out of some forgotten Victorian book: a solid spire rooted to a dark hill. I imagined the sea smashing on distant islands, clouds racing over Mt. Desert toward the western mountains, and, straight up, the full moon, the stars, galaxies, the ultimate forever.

There would be no neighbors near this tower with their petty busynesses and no petty busynesses of my own either. And no distracting black flies or mosquitoes (which is quite an omission in buggy Maine, but I recall that Wordsworth left bugs out of his nature rhapsodies, too). Just me and the wild turkeys, coyotes, moose, porcupines, skunks, deer, eagles, and black bears. Uncompromised. At full attention. Lifted up. Nearer to the eternal spirit. Brother of Thoreau. Child of Holly.

Or maybe just a middle-aged guy in his version of a boy's tree house. I once tacked up such a tree house as a twelve-year-old in suburban Philadelphia. At first, it was going to be an underground bunker ten feet into the earth. I'd conduct elaborate chemical experiments down there and read secret books and keep notes on arcane subjects. But pushing a shovel into the resisting ground a few times convinced me that climbing up into the trees was easier than hunkering down under them.

So I went ten feet the other way, tacked together an anthology of scrap lumber, about five feet by seven feet, and nailed it into the branches of an old mulberry tree. From my platform I studied my neighbors' backyard swing sets and a small woods behind our house. I plastered the trees in the woods with signs — NO HUNT-ING ALLOWED. PREDATOR HUNTING OK — and signed them "The Henderson Game Commission." What I meant was, You can kill the mean foxes and crows, but spare the bunnies and deer. Moral messages for a minuscule forest. Never mind that the last deer had disappeared years ago and there was little left to hunt. My posters flapped in an empty woods. Soon the woods disappeared. A housing development wiped out even the remaining bunnies.

Or maybe I was trying to reconstruct the observation tower in Valley Forge Park. One moonlit night my first girlfriend, Sally, and I climbed over the fence with the CLOSED. KEEP OUT sign and clambered up the metal stairs to the top deck for a view over the entire Revolutionary War campground.

Sally and I called ourselves poets. We would write about Washington and his troops in the cruel snow and about what had happened to America since then. We were sixteen-year-olds with a truth mission.

Patrolling park cops spotted the car at the foot of the tower and skewered us above with their search-light. We were ordered down and arrested "for trespassing after hours."

"We just wanted to write poetry," Sally and I sang together.

The cops smirked. One of them asked, "How old is she?"

"Honest. That's all," I declared indignantly.

Something about my fervor convinced him we were not worth the trouble of handcuffing and transporting to the judge. Instead, he handed me a ticket.

On the way back to her house, Sally and I planned our courtroom defense oratory. We had a patriotic right to free speech, to be in the park after the tourists left, to seek the essence of Washington's suffering troops in the quiet moonlight. And we had only kissed a little.

But we were never summoned, our fine speeches never delivered. The cop threw away the ticket.

Was this the nostalgic reason for my tower now? Did I want to re-create the rebellious glory of that night with Sally?

Maybe it was just youth itself I sought. The artist Rockwell Kent, an amateur builder like myself, constructed and later restored his own cottage on Monhegan Island, Maine, not that far from Sedgwick. He admitted, in 1947, that "all the world has changed; and it is by studied self-delusion made possible by the remoteness of the little house—and without a telephone, electric light and radio, its un-modernity—that I re-live my youth, or better, become young again."

Lost tree house, tower, youth? Why analyze this mania to death? "No reason at all" was still fine with me.

A greater problem was vertigo. Until now, in my dreaming, I had ignored this neurotic malfunction. As a kid, I could scramble up any tree without a care, but now I couldn't climb open stairs a few stories without clawing for support and inching back down on my hands and knees. The vistas from the tops of the great steeples and monuments of Europe and America were unknown to me.

My vertigo was not of the dizzy variety. It was worse. I had topple-down vertigo. At heights I was driven to pitch myself forward into the air.

Unless drunk. Then I was glorious, could endure any altitude. In my debauched thirties I once tiptoed along the parapet of an eight-story New York apartment-house roof, sodden, fearless, and laughing. But that wouldn't help me now. Drunks are no good at making anything.

I'd have to deal with the vertigo some other way. I had no idea what way. That could wait while I handled more immediate difficulties, like building alone.

Because I couldn't afford to pay for help, and my wife was no builder and had no interest in towers of any ilk, I was going to be one guy alone with lots of lumber and cement to haul into the woods, which as yet had no road, no driveway, not even a path. And after I chose my site and assembled my materials, I would have to raise it all alone, and by hand.

I vowed there would be no power tools at this tower. As at the island cottage, my tools would be hammer, handsaw, Tri-Square, tape measure, and level, plus a rope to hold boards while I got a nail into them. That rope would be my only pal.

As for electricity, a line through the sweet woods from the poles at the dirt road? Never. No television, no computer, no E-mail, no fax, no phone. I would be blessedly out of the hypnotic national electronic loop.

And no gasoline machinery, either. No generators, no backhoes, no cranes, I pledged. Bad enough that I drove that smoking Oldsmobile. Someday, it too would go. Then I would rediscover my feet by hiking up and down this magnificent hill.

THOOR BALLYLEE

Simplify, simplify," said Thoreau about building his Walden Pond cabin, and a few paragraphs later he repeated: "Simplify, simplify, simplify." Note: to be truly simple, he might have said the word just once.

For me, his principle of hut design applied to towers, too—at least to my rustic structure. I had imagined fancier towers—an octagonal or a round spire would have offered less wind resistance at the top of Christy Hill, where several large trees had been snapped off by storms. And local stone might have been cheaper and more in the tradition of ancient towers.

But I was a novice architect. Having made up my island cottage as I went along, I understood basic stick framing and rectangular dimensions. This hilltop was no place to experiment with forms or materials and see my creation pitch to earth at the first gust.

I went with what little I knew. In the dimensions of the ten-by-twelve-foot bedroom of my cottage, I discovered my model—an area of reasonable size, almost square (I'd fiddle it to a proper square later), and not so large that a construction with this footprint might be mistaken for a small house. It was also roomy enough for steep stairs or a ladder into the upper chambers. Most crucially, the base would be wide enough to ensure some sort of stability, as long as that base remained firmly anchored to the ground.

Simple. A box on top of a box, and, if I were daring, yet another box on top of that box and so forth into the clouds. Sort of a plain Quaker tower—although, as far as I knew, Quakers erected no towers. I admired the unembellished austerity of Quaker meetinghouses and the Quakers themselves, who sat in silence, for the most part, and let God do the quiet talking.

Later I would discover that William Butler Yeats shared an appreciation for boxed simplicity in his tower, Thoor Ballylee, the one derided by Ezra Pound as "a phallic symbol on the bogs."

Thoor Ballylee stands not in the bogs but by a rushing stream in County Galway, Ireland, about twenty miles inland from the Atlantic Ocean. Yeats bought this Norman-era semi-ruin in 1917 for thirty-five pounds and lived there many summers with his wife, Georgina, and their children. The floors of all the rooms had rotted away and the slate roof had been blasted off by the winds. Working with a local builder, and determined to retain the tower's original uncluttered Norman lines, Yeats used beams, thick planks, and paving stones from an old mill in his restoration.

He recalled his labor in his poem "To Be Carved on a Stone at Thoor Ballylee":

I the poet William Yeats,
With old mill boards and sea green slates,
And smithy work from the Gort forge
Restored this tower for my wife George
And may these characters remain
When all is ruin once again.

The bottom floor, with "great wide windows opening over the river," became the Yeats family dining room, and it doubled as Yeats's study, where he often wrote by candlelight into the night. The next two floors were bedrooms, and the top chamber, named the Stranger's Room, was meant for meditation but was never finished.

All four floors were connected by a winding staircase, which became Yeats's symbol for "the widening gyre" up the stairs of consciousness. In his 1932 collection *The Winding Stair and Other Poems*, he announced:

> *I declare this tower is my symbol: I declare*
> *this winding, spiring treadmill of a stair*
> *is my ancestral stair,*
> *That Goldsmith, the Dean, Berkeley and Burke*
> *have travelled here.*

Thoor Ballylee was not only a symbol for Yeats. It also sheltered his family from the Irish Civil War around him. One night the IRA blew up the stone bridge over his stream and warned Yeats and his family not to leave their tower.

In his "Prayer for My Daughter," Yeats wrote in his dining room/study as the civil war raged and "the seawind scream[ed] upon the tower." He prayed for his child sleeping above him; he asked for the gifts of

Yeats's tower [*Russell Washburn*]

beauty, intelligence, charm, constancy, and "radical innocence."

It was not the IRA that finally drove Yeats from the tower in 1928 but the continual flooding of the stream and the dampness of the stone. It would remain the central image of his later poetry:

An ancient bridge and
A more ancient tower,
A farmhouse that is sheltered by its wall
An acre of stony ground.

Unlike the Norman Thoor Ballylee, my tower would claim for itself nothing that was ancient, except the stony ground it would stand on and this immense slope named for an unknown Christy—a diminutive of the name given someone who died two thousand years ago, a worshiped, demeaned, distant figure who was tortured, nailed down, and lifted up against the sky, asking his father why he had forsaken him.

Someday, the same forces that raised this hilltop would no doubt reduce my tower and Yeats's and all others to "ruin once again."

DUMPSTER DIVING

Because I had spent my advance money on the 1.78 acres, I had little cash for building materials. Like Yeats and Thoreau, I saved by shopping for leftovers—in my case, at yard sales, dumps, and Dumpsters.

Like Thoreau, I kept a detailed record of my acquisitions, free and purchased. In *Walden*, Thoreau wrote: "I have always endeavored to acquire strict business habits: they are indispensable to every man." Later, he listed his expenses:

The exact cost of my house, paying the usual price for such materials as I used, but not counting the work, all of which was done by myself, was as follows . . . :

Boards	$8.03½,	mostly shanty boards.
Refuse shingles for roof and sides	4.00	
Laths	1.25	
Two second-hand windows with glass	2.43	
One thousand old brick	4.00	
Two casks of lime	2.40	That was high.
Hair	0.31	More than I needed.
Mantle-tree iron	0.15	
Nails	3.90	
Hinges and screws	0.14	
Latch	0.10	
Chalk	0.01	
Transportation	1.40	} I carried a good part on my back.
In all	$28.12½	

Not only Yeats and Thoreau used leftovers—one of the great contemporary towers was erected in 1980 by Henry Lueher in the town of Pettibone, North Dakota (population: 93), with materials from a grain elevator he had torn down. Lueher was sixty years old when he started his tower. It evolved over many years into an eight-story octagonal pagoda, peaked by an onion dome shingled with discarded aluminum printing plates.

Lueher, who died a few years ago, designed the interior of his eighty-foot tower with a magpie's taste — shattered phonograph records, discarded toys, rotary-dial telephones, and old calendars. At each floor, he extended a balcony and installed a ladder to the next floor. A trapdoor in the roof led to a sweeping view of the North Dakota prairie.

When asked the reason for his tower, Lueher replied: "I had all this damned lumber around here and I wanted to pile it up. So I piled it up."

Like Thoreau, Yeats, and Lueher, I was cheap with my economies and those economies determined my design. At a Hamptons yard sale, a local builder was trying to unload four windows, 3' wide and 4' 9" high, with real wood partitions between the panes (rare these days — fake snap-on partitions typically divide the glass into separate panes). The price for these classic old windows — ten dollars each. I stored them in the garage for transport to Maine in the spring and I dreamed my top-floor design around them.

Early in March, while bicycling the dead East Hampton resort streets, I came across a Dumpster with sections of a sliding glass door sticking out. Broken

glass, I thought, but braked for a look. The glass wasn't even scratched, just not sliding anymore. Too much trouble to fix. The two thermal-paned panels, 3' 2" wide and 6' 7" high, were free to the scavenger.

I returned with the Oldsmobile and inched them up and out. Very tough to do. Thermal-pane doors are heavy, from 80 to 125 pounds a panel. But since they often refuse to slide, they are common in Dumpsters. And they are terrific fixed tower windows, if you can haul the panels to your car and to the site without developing a hernia or a slipped disk.

My hauling dictum is that if you can move an object a few feet you can move it a mile, if you take your time, rest a lot, and drag slowly. That's how I transported the non-sliding glass-door sections from the Dumpster to the car to the garage to Maine.

Try to forget the influence of our electronic now-now age. Never hurry. If you do, you risk making serious mistakes and hurting yourself so badly that your tower-raising days will be quickly done. Once, rushing, I smashed my forehead on a ladder protruding off the Olds's roof rack and ended up on the ground, cut and dazed. Rushing another time, I tried to budge a boulder by hand rather than searching for a 2" × 4"

Henry Lueher's tower [*Bismarck Tribune*]

lever. The rock rolled backward, smashing my right hand on another rock. It took a year for the fingernails to grow back. I marveled at the fifty-four-year-old stored-up wisdom of my body, which remembered to grow nails so slowly and so perfectly.

Because of my good fortune at the yard sale and the Dumpster—a savings of about two thousand dollars in windows—my design evolved into a tower of light. Ancient defensive spires omitted windows, but I resolved to build for the sun, keeping in mind the obvious need for strength. Light became my essential rule—along with simplicity, frugality, and patience.

For the rest of the winter, I continued to bike from humble Springs to the beach dwellings of the fabulously wealthy, seeking castoffs. Some of the Hamptons mansions were concocted by famous architects and cost millions. One was sided in stainless steel; another, swathed in gray stucco, resembled a skin-diseased bank. That year gables seemed to be in fashion, the more gables the fancier the house, dozens of them popping up at every angle. Curving roofs, too, striving for that "olde English" look; no straight-down slopes here.

And huge was necessary if you were anybody. A giant dwelling announced a big score in the stock market or in some media scam. (So far, the record is a planned 100,000-square-foot sand-dune monstrosity with twenty-nine bedrooms and thirty-two full bathrooms—hotly protested by owners of nearby smaller summer palaces).

Whatever their pretensions, these see-and-be-seen statements have usurped some of the most fertile farmlands on earth. Like an ostentation of peacocks, they stare at each other across treeless lawns, crying "Look at me! Look at me!"

They are tossed up by the dozens every year, but, however new at their throwing up, they become yesterday's news soon after, like last season's New York party dresses.

Ezra Pound may have been wrong about Yeats's tower, but he was right about great literature as "news that stays news." To paraphrase him a bit: lasting structures should stay news, too. The one feature that ensures this, in my unschooled opinion, is ever-changing, always-revealing light.

HANGING STONES IN THE SKY

Many writers hope their creations will last for a few years; indeed some long for immortality. Tower builders seem to have the same passion.

Yeats thought his words and maybe his tower would endure. And I, too, hoped that if I made it well and the storms were forgiving, my tower would outlast me, and perhaps the books I wrote and published would, too. This latter desire is foolish: perhaps 95 percent of the volumes published go out of print during the author's life and almost all are utterly lost in time.

Writers hunger for the luck of Melville, his fictions forgotten at his death and rediscovered and immortalized a few decades later. But for most of us this will not happen.

The poet Robinson Jeffers (1887–1962) longed for immortality, and he was also one of the great amateur tower builders of our time. If his poems didn't last, maybe his tower would, he hoped. He surpassed even Yeats in his passion, constructing his tower single-handedly.

He was a scavenger too, of sorts. His source was the beach outside his home, Tor House, in Carmel, California, which he also built himself. On that beach he found stones, left over from some ancient clash of sea and land, and he hauled them up the cliff to his site.

Jeffers said his inspiration for raising the tower was his wife, Una. She was fascinated by the mysterious Round Towers found throughout Ireland. In creating a rough imitation of these towers, Jeffers designed and labored for her.

He recalled Una's muse in his poem "Angry at the Sun."

> *I built her a tower when I was young—*
> *Sometime she will die—*
> *I built it with my hands, I hung*
> *Stones in the sky.*

In the early 1920s Jeffers was educated in the art of stone construction by local masons. He imagined that the masons, like the poet, were "fighting time with marble." For five years, his immense job of hauling rocks from the beach fifty feet up that cliff, via a wooden chute, was a "far sweeter toil" than writing.

When he finished, he named his forty-foot-high, four-story primitive creation Hawk Tower, for the sparrow hawk that had perched daily on his scaffold. In "Ghost," he described what he had done:

> *There is a jaggle of masonry here, on a small hill*
> *Above the gray-mouthed Pacific, cottages*
> *And a thick-walled tower, all*
> *Made of rough sea-rock*
> *And Portland cement.*

At the peak of Hawk Tower, Jeffers inscribed in stone for future visitors: "R.J. suis manibus me turrem falconis fecit" (With his own hands R.J. made me, tower of the falcon).

From that marble-paved parapet, Jeffers viewed the rural Monterey countryside around him: "For the first time in my life I could see people living—amid

Hawk Tower [*John H. Gamble/Tor House Foundation*]

magnificent unspoiled scenery—essentially as they did in the Idyls or Sagas or in Homer's Ithaca. Here was life purged of its ephemeral accretions. Men were riding after cattle, or plowing the headland, hovered by white sea gulls, as they have done for thousands of years, and will for thousands of years to come."

Like me, Jeffers was the son of a religious man. His father was a professor of biblical languages and ecclesiastical history. According to his wife, Jeffers experienced a sort of mystical conversion after his father died in 1914—he began to worship stone as a symbol of eternity. In "Star Swirls" he wrote:

> *The tower at least will hold against the sea's*
> *buffeting*
> *It will become geological, fossil permanent.*

And from "Harder than Granite":

> *Only the little tower,*
> *Four-foot-thick walled and useless*
> *May stand for a time.*
> *That and some verse.*

Yeats and Jeffers may have remembered that they built their towers for their wives, but clearly, to them and to us, they had something more complicated in mind.

I cannot claim that my charming wife, Annie, inspired my tower. She was not the reason for it. In fact, she wisely preferred that I remain wedded to the earth.

PLAGUE

In the months before I discovered my lot on Christy Hill, a plague of cancers suddenly descended on several of my friends, all of them young women. Their suffering devastated their families and all of us. Who could have faith in a universe that allowed this? Their agony was one of the reasons I had to lose myself in raising the tower. It became a tower of oblivion. Building, I didn't have to think constantly of horror, outrage, and terror.

My friend Kim was thirty-eight, kind, dark-haired, lovely, and the mother of three children — two girls, aged three and five, and a boy, eight. She had met her husband, Ken, when she was a student at Barnard and he at Columbia. After graduating, they married and moved to Southampton. He started a construction company and Kim worked as a personal care nurse.

Ken had almost finished building a house for his family when Kim's headaches started. An operation revealed an aggressive type of brain cancer. Doctors gave her a year at the most.

Kim knew the odds. She had witnessed her own patients die from this cancer. But for her kids and her husband, she never thought of quitting. The pain was constant, the five additional operations excruciating. She allowed herself to be used as a guinea pig for massive chemotherapy doses, without effect. A few months before she died, defying her cancer one last time, she ran, biked, and swam in a triathlon along the local roads and in the bay. At her death, she lay blind and unable to move, surrounded by her family, in the bedroom of the new house that Ken had just completed for her.

Kim had directed that no mention of God or religion be permitted at her funeral. Instead, in a hall packed with mourners, her friends recited her favorite words by Laurie Colwin, Anne Raver, E. B. White, and Kathleen Norris, and sang her favorite songs. As we filed out we all received Kim's final gift to us, a bar of the See's chocolate that she loved.

When I first heard of Kim's cancer, I hit the floor, pleading with the old God of my father's church. "This kind of thing just can't happen to anybody so young, so good. Her kids need her, her husband is wrecked," I explained to this God. I hadn't prayed since I was an adolescent.

On my knees I tried to think of a deal for this old God, the one who parted the Red Sea, whose Son healed the leper and raised Lazarus. The pal of Oral Roberts, Pop's radio healer. I pleaded: "If you heal Kim, I will become a born-again Christian and dedicate my life to your church. No questions asked."

There. My cards were on the table. It was the only thing I could think of. I waited for an answer of some sort. Silence.

When I stood up I felt dirty. I had just treated that God as though he were a car salesman hankering for a deal. I was suddenly appalled by my prayer, and then terrified by what may have been a degrading blasphemy of the very God I was beseeching. I resolved to pray no more. After four decades without much praying, I had forgotten how to pray in any case. What would come of my attempt to reach God? I endured a low-grade fever of dread.

A few months later, an answer of sorts: My brother Bob called me from Philadelphia. He said his wife, Debbie, forty-four, an artist, teacher, and community leader, mother of their two children, a boy fourteen and a daughter eighteen, had also just been diagnosed with brain cancer. It wasn't the aggressive strain that was quickly killing Kim, but, as Debbie's doctor said, "It kills you in the end."

Debbie was operated on at the University of Pennsylvania Hospital. She was left partially paralyzed on her left side, unable to walk without assistance, and doomed to spend her days on the living room couch in front of the TV, swallowing dozens of pills daily, doped and bloated. Bob slept on a rug on the floor by her side, in constant attendance.

"Don't let them do this to you, Bill," she told me after her operation. She also joked that she would outlive her surgeon, who drove a new orange Porsche, purchased, she assumed, with fees from that operation.

Was this God's answer to my botched prayer?

When I told Annie about the deal I had offered God and the result, she observed dryly: "That makes you pretty important, doesn't it?"

Annie was mystified by me and losing patience with our constant poverty. We had been through many bad patches before, but this was starting to look like the end. I slept on the couch every night, alone and miserable.

Annie was right of course. How ridiculous to think my feeble prayer and Debbie's cancer were related, and how egomaniacal.

Kim, who became a hero to me, consoled Debbie by phone. Listless from chemotherapy and radiation treatments, Debbie had tired of talking to her desperate, helpless brother-in-law and friends, but for hours she discussed new chemicals and drugs, doctors, and all the exotica of brain cancer, with Kim.

When I offered what little solace I knew of to Kim, it was Kim who tried to cheer me up. Wearing a scarf to cover her bald head but looking just as young and alert as before her first operation, she held my hand: "Bill, we are all dying. I'm just getting there a little faster than the rest of us."

Every day became incredibly precious to Kim and Debbie. Dying, they loved living with an intensity that we healthy sorts lacked, and I lacked even more as ghastly news arrived of more friends' cancers: the young mother of one of Holly's best friends had colon cancer; another family friend had breast cancer. By the end of the year, three more women friends, all of them vital, good people, were diagnosed with various cancers.

What was the meaning of this grotesque chronology of misery? My huckster's prayer had nothing to do with it, of course, of course. But I didn't dare whisper a plea to heaven, even a plea for forgiveness for my original prayer.

As Simone Weil said in her own dark night, God was "more absent than a dead man, more absent than light in the utter darkness of a cell."

Two years earlier I might have sought solace for my decaying marriage and my dying friends in the little Presbyterian church down the highway. But now it seemed only a weird collection of bickering, deluded hypocrites whose greatest spiritual victory had been videotaping my friend, the Bishop of Blarney, in his bathrobe.

Sudden episodes of pure horror swept over me. Perhaps Yeats's rough beast, its "gaze blank and pitiless as the sun," was no longer slouching toward Bethlehem to be born. The beast had already arrived, indeed had always been in Bethlehem.

Holly's love might not be at the heart of the universe. Something terrible might be, and I was just beginning to see its malevolent face.

I was losing my balance in a new, more virulent form of vertigo. I had to do something just to remain standing on the ground. The "tower for no reason" became that something.

A SITE

March in Down East Maine was gray and brown and of little comfort to me when I drove there to look for a tower site. Nothing could have been more lifeless, not a sprig of green anywhere. Most of the birds were long gone, leaving only gulls, blue jays, chickadees, and noisy crows. "Crow weather" the locals call it.

The first sign of renewal was the ice breaking out of Sedgwick Harbor. John Cole, the veteran Maine nature writer, described such a magic moment:

"In the first week of March, overnight, a ribbon of water ran through the ice from our shore across the cove. At first it was more a string than a ribbon — a thin line of gray against the white ice. It widened to a ribbon after one warm morning, became a sliver of open water just too wide to jump, although no one could tell how it had grown, so slowly did the widening take place . . . the water ribbon became a breaking place. The acres of ice on the bay side of the gap began to move away, to slip down the bay with the first nudges of the falling tide . . . even as the ice moved, the birds returned."

The March temperature on Christy Hill averaged in the forties during the day and the twenties at night, enough heat to thaw the ground a bit and let me start to dig my foundation once I had my site.

Since my little lot was the middle portion of a three-part subdivision, it was possible that at some dim, distant date I would have neighbors, but how close would any neighbor want to come to my tower? There was plenty of land for everybody. I saw only what I wanted to see — an empty hilltop, all my own.

I visited the Sedgwick Town Office, a small wooden structure at the bottom of the hill, to ask about codes and permits. I was prepared to fill out many forms and pay several fees. My visit was brief. The lady in charge said: "Well, we had a meeting a while back about all that, permits, setbacks, and such, but none would have it. So do what you please. Until you plan on flushing, that is. Then you'll need to talk to the plumbing inspector." She gave me his name and phone number.

This was loose, even for Maine. On Deer Isle I had to at least inform the town officials of what I intended to build and get their okay, so they could tax me later. Here, they didn't even want to know what I was up to. I guessed they'd find out soon enough what I had raised and tax it a little. So far the annual land tax was $76.19.

Sedgwick granted me the freedom to erect whatever I liked. Now I only had to seek permission from the wind. If I had been thinking clearly, my model should have been the Eiffel tower, that 945-foot marvel of wind resistance. But that tower had become such a clichéd image of Paris that I didn't bother to consider the lessons it might offer.

In 1889, the Eiffel Tower was the highest man-made structure ever. No other gigantic spire since then has combined such simple grace with such light and lacy strength. In its day, it was a daring gamble and, like all original art, it was derided by some of the pundits of the time as "monstrous," "baroque," "dizzyingly ridiculous," "a gigantic factory chimney." The novelist Guy de Maupassant said he lunched at a restaurant inside the tower so that he wouldn't have to look at it from the outside. In 1906, the Eiffel Tower was almost torn down, until somebody realized it would be ideal for radio signal transmissions.

Alexandre Gustave Eiffel was no amateur or revolutionary builder. He was professionally trained as an engineer and in 1887 started his own iron-fabricating business in Paris, where he designed railroad stations, bridges, and churches that were built around the world. When he dared to suggest a great work of iron for the 1889 Paris Exhibition, he argued that its engineering mastery would prove to the world that "the French are not just an amusing people."

The construction of the Eiffel Tower was in itself a wonder: 14,352 square feet of drawings, 15,000 structural members, 2,500 rivet holes, 1,671 steps to the top, 8,000 tons (that's light—in fact, the entire tower could be squashed into a plate the size of its base, four acres, and it would be only 2½ inches thick). Cost—one and a half million dollars, which, if you were counting, was 5 percent under budget. (Thoreau, with his concern for economy, would have approved of this, and nothing else.)

Eiffel Tower in construction, June 1888. [*Museum of Modern Art/ H. Blancard*]

After two years, two months, and five days in construction, it was completed in time for the Exhibition, and none of the 250 workers was even slightly injured in the process—a fact which amazes me when I remember that I couldn't even hammer up a three-story tower without suffering a gashed forehead and a smashed hand.

I also marvel at Eiffel's skill in obtaining the necessary permits for such a windproof lark. Think of the committees, the politics, the restrictive codes. What a dead hand he lifted! Look at his tower again as if for the first time.

In Sedgwick we have no obvious dead hands. I am sure there are committees and politics lurking about somewhere, but I have yet to stumble upon them. And the only code seems to be "Thou shalt not flush on thy neighbor." (It may be a sad sign that the code is moving beyond mere flushing: a permit is now required for an outhouse, it costs $125, and a plumbing fellow has to come by and inspect your hole!)

So far, what you build and how you choose to live in Sedgwick are mostly your own business. The only job of local government is to keep hands off, unless you are buried in a blizzard or your woodstove burns your house down. Then the whole town turns out to help. In these parts, people need each other. There are no better neighbors anywhere. Community means practically everything.

My only real restriction was in the deed. It said I'd have to create at least a 1,000-square-foot house on the lot someday. This was to be a rural upscale subdivision; no trailers, huts, or wigwams. That irked me, but since there was no time limit, I put off such a shack many years in my mind. However, I would want to place the tower away from any future building. It had to be solitary and self-supporting. No real tower is attached to a house, at least no tower celebrated in this book.

The land sweeping up Christy Hill from ocean and river was rolling and sometimes steep. But my little copse at the top, for some geological reason, was as flat as New Jersey. And, unlike much of the land below, it was marsh free. Building here would be a lot easier than on a slope or in the muck. But the ground was stony, and granite bedrock lay a few feet under the surface at some points, according to the soil test report. Not the easiest stuff to dig up for a foundation.

Hunting for a spot, Opie and I explored the length of the stone wall, he for red squirrels and chipmunks to annoy, I to study views and vegetation. To the west, a few small beeches and various bushes obscured the view. I couldn't cut them since they were over the property line, although no neighbors were visible and I doubted if anybody would care. At one place, the growth was minimal and I decided to build the tower there, close to the wall, as far from the scurrying road as I could get. Traffic up here was light except at blueberry harvest, when I expected an army of pickup trucks and migrant workers.

Also, if the blueberry business went sour, I worried that the ocean field seemed prime for development with its distant view of Acadia National Park and L'Isle des Monts Déserts, as French explorer Samuel de Champlain named Mt. Desert. In those mountains nineteenth-century artists Thomas Cole, Frederick Edwin Church, and other Hudson River School painters found inspiration and were soon followed by rich rusticators like the Rockefellers, Vanderbilts, Pulitzers, and Morgans. A similar migration happened in East Hampton, where Jackson Pollock and William de Kooning led the way for an invasion of the wealthy from New York City.

The hills, lakes, and forests of 40,000-acre Acadia swarm with visitors now, but from here I saw not a person. There was only the eternal quiet of the sort that inspired Rockwell Kent to paint Monhegan Island rising from the sea and name the painting *Reverence*.

Close to the wall, about 120 feet from the road and tucked up near the northern boundary, seemed about right for my site. Any potential neighbor wouldn't build right on the line with all this room, would he? Unlikely. This forest might remain undisturbed for hundreds of years, I guessed, and I would bother it as little as possible. Who else would want to live in this howling wilderness? This was a dangerous place. In the winter the ice and snow might trap you up here for weeks. There would never be development here, in the fields, or next door, I concluded.

I cleared out a few small trees and marked my ten-by-twelve-foot dimensions with string and stakes. With a minimum of tree-cutting, I'd have an unobstructed view of the sunrise over Acadia's Cadillac Mountain in the east and of the sunset over what I thought was Mt. Katahdin in the west, almost seventeen hours of daylight at midsummer.

I put a foot to the shovel.

PISA

As a Sunday school child, I was taught that you should begin your life on a firm foundation: on rock, not sand; on wisdom, not ignorance; on righteousness, not sin. Before I had any idea of what a foundation was, I sang the words of a hymn: "The church's one foundation is Jesus Christ our Lord . . ." I learned to be obsessed with a proper

Leaning Tower of Pisa [*CORBIS/Bettmann-UPI*]

foundation and to expect the rewards of such a base in heaven.

Only later did I hear about the citizens of Pisa, Italy, and how a lousy foundation on their 193-foot tower made them rich, if not saintly.

The Leaning Tower of Pisa leaned almost from the start. In 1174 Bonanno ("Good Year") started piling blocks, and he was up to the third balcony of his project when a local war stopped him. Building resumed ninety-eight years later, in 1272, but the tower was already tilting toward the south. To fix this, the engineers of the time tilted the next floors slightly to the north, (a bend you notice today). But this didn't help. The tower continued to tilt more and more, about ⅕ of an inch to the south each year.

In Galileo's day, it was fifteen feet off plumb. That's why he dropped things from its top balcony to his daughter. By 1990 it leaned so badly that it was closed to visitors—about 800,000 a year, netting the city over two million dollars. As recently as 1997, a group of international experts proposed strapping steel suspenders to its middle and anchoring them to stone supports, an indignity that Pisans resented. They told the experts that the tower could take care of itself, as it had for centuries. And they noted that the last time the so-called experts tried to fix the tower, it tilted ⅒ of an inch in just one night.

The cause of Pisa's lean is in the subsoil, and the blame rests on Bonanno, who didn't check his dirt before laying that first block. Of course, if he had raised a straight-up tower, nobody today would fuss much about this lovely round object. We are fascinated by Pisa the way race-car fans are enthralled by the Indy 500. We await the crash.

If Bonanno had known what was under him, he wouldn't have bothered. The soil under Pisa is a complicated mix: for thirty-three feet down it is sandy muck; for the next seventy feet it's hard clay and sand; from there on down it's water-saturated sand. Not promising for a 14,000-ton tower.

Except for its tilt, Pisa is similar to the hundreds of other towers the Italians built in this period. It is made of an outer cylinder of heavy stone blocks, an inner cylinder of porous, weaker stone, and an interior fill of stone chips—all of this surrounded by a facade. Here, Pisa is unique. Its facade is marble—not brick. Also, it's round, and not square as were most towers. Pisa's wraparound balconies are unique, too. Long ago, when Pisa was a great maritime power, and before the sea retreated six miles, you could climb the 294 clockwise steps to the top balcony and survey the ships below you in the harbor.

But what people admired most was not the facade or the round design of the balconies but the tilt. In fact, the builders of Bologna designed their 321-foot Torre degli Asinelli (Tower of the Little Donkeys) to lean slightly. Tilt was chic, just as perfectly plumb is cool in our time, except for old buildings that are admired today for their exhausted, antique sag.

The Italians love their towers (yet another reason why I admire the Italians). One small town, San Gimignano, once decorated with seventy-two towers, now has only about fifteen standing. The world's tallest brick tower is in Siena, the 334-foot Torre del Mangia, so named because its bell ringer loved to eat. You can see a copy of it in Provincetown, Massachusetts.

To the Italians, towers were a matter of family honor. If a rival family decided a clan's tower was climbing too high, they slighted it. Here's how: the rising tower was propped with poles, strategic bricks removed, the poles burned, and the tower was destroyed. (In Maine, I was told of similar direct action against an offending structure. A local boy, miffed that a new house was going up in his favorite dirt-bike field, simply burned it down.)

And then again, God seemed to have had a hand in tower slighting. The Campanile de San Marco, the bell tower for St. Mark's in Venice, begun in 888, was toppled by lightning in 1902. And restored. The Civic Tower of Pavia, "the town of 100 towers," standing firmly since 1060, collapsed without warning at 8:55 a.m., on March 17, 1989, killing four people. No groans, rumbles, shrieks. No hint at all. "It just disappeared," said one eyewitness.

Every tower builder worries about that one.

My foundation of choice on Christy Hill was cement posts. These posts would be positioned about four feet deep into the hardscrabble, three pillars on the east side and three on the west.

Another possibility I briefly considered, and rejected, was a professionally poured cement slab, more expensive by far and therefore out of the question since I was laying this foundation cheaply and by myself. Also, transporting wet cement to the site would have required hacking out a rough 120-foot driveway, dumping truckloads of gravel for a sub-foundation, and creating general havoc in the woods with a backing, turning, pouring, roaring cement truck.

Cement posts are terrific foundations for the amateur builder. These posts can be created anywhere. All that is required is a strong back or a sturdy wheelbarrow, a shovel, and buckets.

The builder will also need the following materials:

1. Waxed cardboard tube forms.

    In Maine, these forms are called Sonotubes, but they are manufactured elsewhere under different brands. The tubes come in varying diameters and lengths and can be easily cut to the desired height.

2. Premixed concrete.

    Bags of Portland cement, sand, and aggregate already sifted together and ready to mix with water and pour into the tube.

3. Rebars and J-bolts.

    A rebar (reinforcing bar) is a metal rod that is plunged into the just-mixed-and-poured concrete as it stands in the tube, which in turn stands in the hole you have just dug. I used four shafts of rebar per tube and at the top of each tube I sunk a J-bolt that protruded from the top of the post and would hold the main girder to that post.

When I started to dig the first hole for my six posts, I discovered that the soil, unbuilt upon since perhaps

Civic Tower of Pavia [*Matthys Levy/Kevin Woest*]

forever, was not interested in my tower vision. The shovel would not penetrate the top layer of tangled roots and rocks. I took a hammer to it, then an ax and shovel, to chop away the roots. An hour later, hammer, ax, and shovel had progressed only two feet into the ground.

The local wisdom at the Sedgwick General Store was that a four-foot depth was minimal on Christy Hill. The ground sometimes froze deeply there. Four feet got you below the frost line and prevented frost heaves from forming under the posts and moving them every which way. I was at two feet, sweating, exhausted, with five holes to go.

Soon I was dredging up only a pittance of cracked rock, no matter how hard I hammered, chopped, and dug. No tower would rise here if this continued. I retreated to the general store for a cup of coffee and a reassessment of plans.

On the store bulletin board, a backhoe and driver were advertised for fifty dollars an hour. I wavered awhile, staring into my coffee cup, while I debated my "no machines" rule. Then I bent. If I could protect the woods from the backhoe's ravages and save the tower, the fifty dollars was a bargain.

I called for help.

Dave Webb arrived later that afternoon with his huge backhoe on a trailer towed behind a mammoth earth-moving dump truck. It turned out Dave was a member of the Sedgwick Town Planning Board. Like all Maine tradesmen I met, he was eager to help and talk.

We talked black bears (dangerous only if with cubs . . . and by the way, did I know their call was like the hoot of an owl?), moose (Dave said somebody had found droppings on Little Deer Isle, where supposedly no moose were), and coyotes (a couple of them visited his neighbor's lawn and took a dump in front of his kenneled dogs, just to insult them, it seemed).

We walked through the woods to my problem.

"A tower," Dave mused. "Gets breezy up here."

He said no more. This was my project.

But he did have some information for me. This was one of the highest points on the east coast, bettered only by the mountains of Mt. Desert. That's why, during World War II, the Navy had built a now-deserted concrete-block radar station a mile up the dirt road in the middle of blueberry fields.

I learned later from Rachel Carson's *The Edge of the Sea* that Christy Hill was really the peak of an ancient mountain that was partially submerged when a glacier sank eastern Maine and Nova Scotia as much as 1,200 feet: "All of the northern coastal plain was drowned . . . none of it remains above the sea except here and there a high isolated hill."

Dave and I decided that he would dig two parallel trenches, each four feet deep. I would then settle my cardboard tubes in the trenches at the correct intervals, fill them with cement mix, rebars, and J-bolts, backfill the earth with a shovel, and be ready to fasten my two main 6" × 6" pressure-treated Southern pine girders atop them after the cement cured.

We uncovered a faint natural path, perhaps a farm road long ago, relatively treeless. Through this path, Dave powered his backhoe, obliterating bushes and a pretty twenty-foot fir that got in his way. A monster was loose in my woods and I couldn't wait for Dave to finish and retreat.

His claw ripped into the soil and within minutes he had two trenches halfway scooped out. Then, at 2½ feet, the land started to screech in protest against his metal fangs. It would yield no more than pebbles. We had hit bedrock.

"Decayed granite," as Dave put it. He could do no more with his machine than I had done by hand—a lesson I pondered, and held on to.

We regarded the trenches, studied the insides of our hats, talked some more.

"Black flies in a month or so," I mentioned.

"That's for sure," Dave agreed.

"As soon as it hits sixty."

"About that."

I paid him the fifty dollars, and he reloaded his backhoe on the trailer and roared off down the hill.

Quiet returned. And profound frustration. I sat on the pile of dirt and stared at my useless trenches and felt bad about the murdered fir. I took a long walk with Opie down and up the hill. Halfway back, Opie thought it vital that he dig a hole at the roadside. He scratched up a small pile and forgot about it for more pressing nose business. Looking at the pile I realized the simple solution: If I couldn't get below 2½ feet, I'd pile up the earth 1½ feet around each post and achieve my four-foot burial. That should do it for the frost heaves. Dave had left plenty of loose dirt. The next day I'd get started.

An overnight wet snow squall that would continue off and on all day had covered Dave's dirt and our trenches. The cold weather would be of no help in curing the concrete either, but by urgent phone request from Holly, I was due back on Long Island. I had to pour cement now so that I could begin placement of the girders and joists when I returned later in the spring.

At A.J.'s lumberyard, I selected eight-inch-diameter Sonotubes. I had a pick of larger or smaller diameters, but A.J. said this size might do it for a modest tower. He was still skeptical of my chances of surviving more than a few storms on Christy Hill. "Just make sure when it blows down you're not in it or under it," he reminded me.

With an old saw, I cut each twelve-foot-long tube into three four-foot sections and positioned the sections at equal intervals in the two trenches, three on each side. Using my level and a ten-foot 2 × 4 (eyeballed first for warping) that I placed on the as-yet-empty tubes, I checked for level and added or subtracted soil as necessary, to make them all the same height and still low enough to the ground to keep down my center of balance.

Then it was time for some heavy lifting. The bags of ready-mix Sakrete weighed eighty pounds each, about the lift-limit for one mid-fifties man in relatively good shape. Each post required slightly more than two bags of mix, or fifteen bags total. Since the ground was too rough for a wheelbarrow, my shoulder had to do for the march to the site.

Lifting each bag out of the back of the Olds and onto my right shoulder was dicey. Often I didn't make it to my shoulder and had to let the bag drop back into the car. I developed a ritual of pep talks and deep breathing, followed by a yell. "It's show time!" I'd holler to the gray, indifferent sky—and lift. Now and then I made it to my shoulder. Many "show times!" later I had managed to stagger with more than 1,000 pounds of ready-mix through the snowy woods.

Each sack was followed by a bucket of water. Since there was no nearby pond, I put two 32-gallon garbage cans in the back of the car, filled them with water from the hose at the cottage, and drove the sloshing cans to the top of the hill. From there I hauled the water to my waiting tubes, bucket by bucket.

With a garden trowel, I blended the water and ready-mix in a large plastic tub (procured at the Deer Isle dump) about half a bag at a time, following this recipe: Add a little water and a little mix, stir to the consistency of thick soup, pour into the tube. Repeat until the tube is filled to the brim.

At this point, I added the four sections of four-foot-long ⅜-inch rebar cut for me at A.J.'s lumberyard, spacing them around the inside of each post. And, finally, I pushed the J-bolt into the wet cement for its 8½-inch length, with the top of the bolt protruding, ready to receive the nut and the metal plate that would in turn fasten to the main girder.

By sunset the six Sonotubes were filled with cement, rebarred, J-bolted, and wrapped with individual plastic shopping bags to keep the cement-curing moisture in.

I backfilled only enough dirt around the posts to keep them standing, since I might have to adjust them later in the spring after they settled.

I stationed my two 6" × 6" × 12' girders on the snow next to each line of posts, like a promise to myself. When I returned, the 2" × 6" floor joists would be nailed to these girders and the plywood floor would be attached to the top of the joists.

This would be a terrific foundation, I thought, ready for any tower I chose to fasten to it, however high, and equal to anything nature might throw at it. Certainly better than Pisa's mushy-bottomed effort.

As the March night closed in and the snow squalls finally scudded away toward the Penobscot River, a half-moon rose over the ocean. I cut a few branches to clear a view toward the ocean and that moon. Out on the eastern field a dark shadow moved effortlessly through the dim light into the trees. A big moose.

I didn't tell Opie about the moose and, before he caught its scent and caused a ruckus, I picked him up and, mindful of his dignity, carried him to the car.

We headed south to Holly, Annie, and East Hampton, leaving the cement posts to cure and harden in the early spring, until after the black flies swarmed, feasted on every miserable warm-blooded being, and died by the billions.

The black fly, I concluded, is the miniature cousin of Yeats's rough beast, a bug so vicious that multiple bites can cause fatal allergic reactions and at the very least produce welts that itch and fester for days; a bug that seems to have no use in the food chain, that was created only to spread misery, to mate, to die, and to reappear every spring to continue the cycle of pure buggy evil.

DESPAIR'S ECSTASY

The crocuses bloomed in our East Hampton garden in time for Holly's eleventh birthday on March 14, just the way they had every spring. Holly was excited about the many friends who would be coming to her birthday party.

Despite, or maybe because of, the illnesses of Kim and Debbie and others, I too was in a mood of elation and sudden manic purpose. With Doris Grumbach and our "Founder Emeritus," Henry Thoreau, I had started the Lead Pencil Club to resist the onslaught of electronics—omnipresent computers, faxes, voice mail, and the Internet, all the so-called advances of the superhyped Information Age that promised us a garbage heap of data (and data collection about our personal lives) at lightning speed. This was the same all-powerful big brother I had questioned when I started Pushcart Press to celebrate small presses in the early days of media conglomeration.

The New York Times featured the club's opinions on the Op-Ed page. CBS's *48 Hours* asked for an interview and invaded our home for an afternoon. With an evangelist's voice that I hardly recognized as my own, I glared at the camera and thundered at Gore, Gates, and other cyberpriests. "The information superhighway is nonsense! Power to the pencil!"

For hours I preached to the skeptical interviewer, a Mr. Jones, who kept asking me if I didn't have a secret yen for computers. I said we were speeding to nowhere, that machines were taking over our minds and bodies—a slow suicide—and that we needed human teachers in our classrooms, not teaching machines. I complained about our national mania of impersonal busyness spurred by electronics. "Ask yourself, Mr. Jones," I concluded, "What are people for?"—a reference to Wendell Berry's essential meditation on computers and community, which I doubt Mr. Jones had heard of.

Weeks later the program aired. I got thirty seconds. Two hours of my screed ended up on the cutting-room floor. *48 Hours* lauded technology, using me only as a sound-bite crazy so that CBS could claim a "balanced" presentation. I should have known better than to rise to their bait and feed their agenda. Still, I wondered, where had that evangelist's fire come from? It was as if Billy Graham had hidden in my soul since that 1948 Music Pier born-again conversion with Pop.

At the little Napeague church, I resumed a tentative dance with the Presbyterians. Perhaps, now that my pal the Bishop of Blarney was defrocked, they'd try to heal themselves and to behave as they preached, prayed, and sang.

One Sunday, Rob Stuart, the minister of the nearby Amagansett Presbyterian Church and a friend, visited the pulpit as a temporary fill-in minister. Rob, a gay man, often conducted healing services for AIDS patients and for others who were seriously ill in the community. When Rob asked for prayer requests, I raised my hand on impulse and blurted out that I needed him and the congregation to pray for Kim, Debbie, and my other friends. I had never dared this before. Of what use could such prayers be? Communal mumbo jumbo. Still, since I couldn't pray after my last, disastrous attempt to petition the old God, maybe their prayers would help.

Following the healing prayers, Rob preached about that revolutionary and subversive Christian idea, love your enemies. I enthusiastically joined in the singing of those great old hymns, "Oh God Our Help in Ages Past," "Rock of Ages," and "Fairest Lord Jesus." In those hymns, all of our differences were swept away through song. In his benediction, Rob sent us on our way with instructions "to live transparently as Christians."

I soared out of the tilting-steepled sanctuary renewed in love, wonder, and forgiveness—virtues I badly needed that morning, as Annie had ripped into a rage at me about something and I was set to return rage for rage. (Why is it harder to forgive your spouse than a host of enemies?) Instead of anger, I offered her a kiss.

My sick friends continued to teach me about courage. Kim endured her third brain operation and started training for the triathlon. Debbie, an avowed agnostic, discovered a religious ecstasy in living that was her gift to my brother and me and to all who tried to comfort and care for her.

When I traveled to visit Debbie in suburban Philadelphia that spring, I feared a debilitating depression. The suburbs, where I grew up, were depressing enough—the standard tidy lawns and expensive houses side by side. To see my brother's young wife dying, part of her brain gone, soon to leave him and her children, would be unbearable, I imagined.

But it was Debbie who cheered me up. Although she was swollen from drugs and couldn't walk without assistance, she was the happiest person in the room, just as witty and gracious as ever. She talked of painting again, and teaching, too.

Her grace brought my brother and me closer than we had ever been. While waiting for my train back to New York, we embraced and spoke of our caring for each other, something we hadn't expressed since childhood, if then.

A few weeks before, the mother of Holly's best friend had been operated on at Memorial Sloan-Kettering Hospital in New York. After a five-hour operation, she stayed in the hospital for two weeks and often visited the chapel there. She reported to us that, as she recovered from her pain and fear, one verse from Psalms made all the difference to her: "This is the day the Lord has made. Rejoice and be glad in it."

Einstein said: "There are those who believe nothing is a miracle and others who believe everything is." Einstein came down on the side of everything. Thanks to Holly, Rob, Kim, Debbie, and my friends, I too saw the miracle in everything that spring.

But just on the other side of my manic joy was despair. So much agony, so much dying. As Philip Larkin wrote:

The total emptiness forever
The sure extinction we travel to
And shall be lost in always. Not to be here.
Not to be anywhere,
And soon; nothing more terrible, nothing more true.

One day I woke up to discover a small, strange skin eruption on my chest. My mother had died of breast cancer. Was this that? And what was that sharp twinge in my liver? Too much wine? A sympathy pain for our friend with colon cancer? Pure hypochondria? I was overwhelmed by an epiphany of panic and dread. Cancer had come close and maybe was here now for me. Death was patiently waiting for Holly, Annie, all of us, while I tried to cobble together spiritual pep talks. The universe seemed dead at the core. I couldn't recall what the point had been — love, wonder, forgiveness? Meaningless words to me, suddenly.

From a total Yes, I spiraled down to an absolute No.

I remember fighting back into the light. I recalled the example of my friend Frank Stiffel, who survived Treblinka, the Warsaw ghetto, and Auschwitz, and had written a memoir, *The Tale of the Ring: A Kaddish*, that had been rejected by publishers for forty years. The market was saturated with survivors' accounts, the commercial publishers calculated. I had published Frank's memoir in Pushcart's overlooked manuscript series.

I was in awe of Frank. At the death camps, and in his life in Queens, New York, since then, Frank practiced the kind of gentleness that preachers only preached about. Frank never lost his spirit or his caring. If Frank could endure all that he endured, I certainly could make it past this panic. I concentrated on Frank's name like a mantra.

But I was on the edge of a strange, new precipice.

Soon after the passing shudder of that day, I was reading Reynolds Price's memoir A *Whole New Life*, about his near-fatal cancer of the spine. Price was fifty-one, about my age, and had been sick for a long time when, as he describes it, an "event" with Jesus took place at the Sea of Galilee in Israel. Price, always skeptical of religious sentimentality, insists on that term "event" as something real, not a wish, a dream, or a ghostly visitation.

> I was in my body but was also watching my body from slightly upward and behind. I could see the purple dye on my back, the long rectangle that boxed my thriving tumor.

Jesus silently took up handfuls of water and poured them over my head and back till water ran down my puckered scar. Then he spoke once—"Your sins are forgiven"—and turned to shore again, done with me.

I came on behind him, thinking in standard greedy fashion, "It's not my sins I'm worried about." So to Jesus' receding back, I had the gall to say, "Am I also cured?"

He turned to face me, no sign of a smile, and finally said two words—"That too." Then he climbed from the water, not looking around, really done with me.

I followed him out and then, with no palpable seam in texture of time or place, I was home again in my wide bed.

I set the book aside to ponder this event and the almost miraculous cure that followed it. Through the window I watched Holly playing with her friends. She had grown up so fast. The child she had been was almost gone, and my just-finished memoir had been an epitaph for that child. I knew I was in mourning.

I thought I heard a voice: "Behold I am with you always."

I gasped, "With me always?"

I thought for a moment more. No. Too easy to crank up Jesus Bible verses from boyhood. "Behold?" What kind of lingo was that? But I kept listening. Silence. I decided that, unlike Reynolds Price's "event," my visit from Jesus was a fraud.

BOULDER

In mid-June I left Holly and Annie once again for ten days and, transporting my latest acquisitions from the East Hampton dump—a small, new window with the Andersen sticker still attached, and a slightly battered daybed—I arrived at foggy Christy Hill, and started to haul my treasures to the site.

It had been a cold, miserable June so far in Sedgwick, according to the *Island Ad-vantages* newspaper—ten rainy days and only three with minimal sun. The tiny birch and beech leaves were just out, pale and tender in the white fog. The mosquitoes had arrived on schedule, squadrons of them. They joined the last of the black flies and were all over Opie and me instantly.

I was halfway along the path into the woods when something to the right formed out of the fog. Something very large. Maybe a dead brown tree was my first guess. A few steps farther and I saw it was no tree but a framed and sheathed two-story house-in-progress, with seaside dormer windows, an attached garage, and framing for a rocking-chair porch. This thing was just twenty feet from my property line.

I dropped the daybed and window and leaned against a tree, openmouthed. This was a ferocious woods, the home of bad beasts and killer blizzards. That suburban special over there was impossible, a trick of the fog. I wasn't seeing what I was seeing. It was as if I had just whacked my thumb with a hammer and couldn't believe it until the pain assured me that I had indeed whacked it.

The thing was silent. It lurked there waiting for the morning's workers to arrive and start sawing and slamming on it. Whoever had ordered it erected had cleared most of the lot, removing that portion of the sweet woods. (I found out later it was the dream villa of a jovial Rhode Island policeman and his pleasant wife—good neighbors—who had decided Christy Hill was the perfect retirement spot.)

I trudged back to my hardened and hopeful posts with their upward-protruding J-bolts, ready for the placement of the patiently waiting girders and joists.

If I had raised my tower in this corner, I would have had a stunning view not only of the mountains and ocean but also of my neighbors' upstairs bedroom window, garage, and asphalt driveway. I noticed that footings were in place for a deck out back. I'd be a towering and uninvited witness to many a jolly barbecue there.

I suppose I should have thanked God—if I were in communication with a thankable god then—that I had not yet framed the tower. If I had started it a month or two earlier, this tribute to normalcy next door might have risen in the face of my partially finished glory.

Somebody had given me a second chance to find the correct site. And I had been reminded never to be too hopeful about what can or cannot happen on adjacent vacant land.

Opie and I paced for hours back and forth from road to wall and line to line searching for a tower spot. Our howling wilderness was feeling a bit cramped. The other unbuilt lot on the southern boundary was still for sale. Who knows what might emerge there? It looked as though my deed-dictated future cottage and the tower would be close companions, front yard and backyard, huddled together.

I'd have to begin all over again: digging six holes inch by inch in the rocks and roots, shouldering fifteen bags of eighty-pound cement mix and many buckets of water to a new foundation.

So be it.

In Fellini's 8½, about the chaotic making of a movie and the erection of a tower, an exhausted character, echoing Fellini's sentiments, says, "This tower of mine—what is it?"

Sitting on the tumbled wall, mountains lost in the fog behind me, not bothering to fend off mosquitoes and dying black flies, I was hit with a similar despair.

Why did I need to build this tower? What was the point? What was the point, period? Food for mosquitoes, flies, and worms, I was. Wasn't this tower just a Sisyphean metaphor for enormous effort resulting in zip? "Why am I doing this?" I called into the fog. Opie looked up at me curiously, and then settled into a grumpy snooze. It was hard to smell stuff in the foggy drip.

Then I noticed I had been gazing at a large patch of moss. Oddly, no trees grew out of this mossy area, about ten feet long by eight feet wide. In this tiny forest, trees, most of them malnourished, struggled up in every sparkle of sunlight. Why not here?

With the toe of my shoe, I poked at the moss and pushed it back. Under it was a rock, granite, not decayed—perfect, pristine granite. I lifted the rest of the moss off like a fine rug. Underneath it I discovered a huge boulder, incredibly almost level. This giant was at the very peak of Christy Hill, descending toward the center of the earth, I imagined. It was almost as flat as a builder's cement slab, and almost the measurements of my intended tower.

There had been times when I wondered if somebody or something really is in charge of coincidences like this, synchronicities, as they are popularly called. Just a few months before, a similar event had baffled and terrified me.

For years I had worked on my memoir about my mother, Annie, and me, about Holly's birth and what Holly taught me. I typed endless drafts on an electric typewriter, trying to get it right. Such a typewriter had a ribbon that flat out quit when it was at the end of its spool, unlike the manual typewriter ribbon that rewinds over and over. (I recently switched back to manual.) I was typing the last word of the last sentence of the final draft of that memoir.

I was describing a horrible accident. Holly had been bouncing on her bed in our Deer Isle cottage and had hit her head hard on the wall. We were rushing her to a hospital in Ellsworth.

Annie and I placed her on the back seat. I was certain that at any moment Holly would die from a blood clot as we sped over narrow, blind-crested country roads to the hospital an hour north.

I swore to myself if Holly died I would kill myself. There was no other reason to live. I'd take my chances on finding her again in the afterlife. By night, I too would be dead.

Later, Annie told me she had planned the same for herself.

Then Grace descended.

This was a word I had never thought about before. Grace. I had never experienced it, couldn't even define it.

Grace.

From nowhere, unsought, and inappropriately. My child was dying. I was doing eighty miles an hour. And this thing happened.

I suddenly felt an enveloping love for the entire universe. Not just for my suffering child.

For Annie. For all of it. For all our living and dying.

And I knew I was loved in return. From the very depth of the stars, I was loved.

There would be no suicide, no matter what happened to Holly.

After the CAT scan, the doctor said Holly was OK, and Annie and I collapsed in relief. But in that time I learned a new word.

And Love became palpable.

Love had transcended Holly and Annie and me and infused every pebble on the road as we tore desperately to Ellsworth.

At the "h" on Ellsworth, the ribbon gave up, barely imprinting the period. The odds of this happening at this moment after eight years—at the very end of my manuscript—were infinitesimal. In short, impossible. In shock and fright, I looked at the faded period and simply shrieked. What was that ribbon telling me? This is the truth? Stop here? Write no more?

"What do you want with me?" I yelled at the machine. "Leave me alone!"

Of course, there was no reply. But maybe I already had the answer in that sentence "Love had transcended . . ."

Same for the boulder. This is what I sought! It had been presented to me at the exact center of the property by the old wall, as far from the scampering road as it could be, and on the precise day I needed it most.

Here, nearly 400 feet above sea level, almost as high as the Great Pyramid of Cheops at Giza (which, by the way, took 100,000 men twenty years to pile up), was the archetypal foundation, solid biblical granite.

"Thank you," I murmured to the moss.

MARTELLO TOWER #11

Whether your foundation is a cluster of pillars like the one I left in the dirt or a rock prepared by the big bang billions of years ago, the principles of construction are similar.

I dragged my two girders from the old site to the new. Pressure-treated Southern pine is heavy. It's infused with chemicals I prefer not to think about, guaranteed safe by the manufacturer, of course, unless you burn it and inhale the smoke, or snort the sawdust, or drive a splinter through your hand. In ground contact, or on top of a damp stone, such a rot-and-insect-proof concoction will last "at least 40 years," according to the label. I'd be in my middle nineties before I'd have to haul these girders out and replace them.

Tucking one end of a twelve-foot girder under my arm, I dragged and rested, dragged and rested, trailing swarms of complimentary bugs. When you work on your own project, you can take your time hauling heavy stuff. If you prefer, and like to swat mosquitoes and flies, you can sit on your girder all day and whistle. Someday your tower will rise—if not this month, then the next; if not this summer, then some other summer.

Mostly I dreamed of Holly. She was in the final weeks of her fifth-grade year at the Springs School. What was she doing right now? Was she at her desk? On the playground? Was some teacher bugging her? What was Holly thinking about? Probably a boy. It was getting to be that time. Or maybe her great collection of Pogs, decorated plastic wafers that were suddenly and inexplicably the national rage, as if some Pog Spirit had contacted every child in the middle of the night. Holly had hundreds of Pogs, each different.

By the end of that daydreaming day, the girders were sitting on the big bang boulder, eight feet apart, running east to west. From the Sedgwick post office telephone, I called A.J.'s lumberyard for a morning delivery of 2" × 6" spruce boards for joists and rough exterior plywood for flooring and sheathing.

The next day was, as usual, foggy and drippy. My friend Bill arrived from the lumberyard and we unloaded the boards and plywood, as we had done so often when I was building the Deer Isle cottage. Afterward, we chatted about deer and cars while leaning on his truck. Since there are no pubs in the area, leaning on truck fenders, not bars, serves for male chat.

I tried out my tower plan on him.

Bill didn't quite know what to do with that. Nobody around here had ever come up with such a notion. After a few minutes he was ready with his opinion: "If I had a tower, I'd shoot deer from it."

Bill had been badly disappointed by last fall's hunt. The apple trees dropped their fruit too quickly, and by November the apples had rotted and didn't lure deer as they had in the past. He figured a tower might change his luck.

I switched the subject to cars, bragging that my Olds odometer had just hit 160,000 miles.

"That's nothin'," allowed Bill. "I've got 260,000 on my '70 Buick." He said he'd done all the fixing up himself. The next month, I saw Bill and his souped-up Buick in the Deer Isle Fourth of July parade with the

Model T Fords and ancient farm tractors. That evening he cut a fine figure line-dancing with precision at the Stonington fishing pier.

Bill and I covered the plywood with a tarp against the constant June drizzle, and then we were back on deer and cars.

"Friend of mine hit a deer up near Bangor," he said. "Four-point buck. Looks like it's dead, roadkill. So he slides it into the back of his brand-new Plymouth wagon. Guess what? The deer was only stunned. Kicked out all the glass, the dash, all the inside. Everything. Ruined the wagon. Almost killed him. Kicked his way right out of there and took off."

I signed for the delivery and Bill drove away after a final reminder about my tower and his plans for the November hunt. I said I'd think about that.

I was alone again in the dripping silence.

Every foundation decision I made now was crucial. Since there were no texts on tower construction, I had to guess constantly.

I guessed that my ten-foot 2" × 6" joists would run across the girders and stick out a foot at each side. It didn't seem like much of an overhang at the time, but it made a difference in stability that I would profoundly appreciate while finishing the summit.

I needed that overhang because the boulder was only eight feet wide and I did not want to raise an eight-by-twelve-foot oblong that might be mistaken for a skinny whatever. Towers are square, octagonal, or round, by tradition. With the overhang, I was at ten-by-twelve, only two feet from square. (Later, a balcony would achieve my almost perfect square.) Why the square tradition? I have no idea.

On the abandoned pillar foundation, the girders would have been attached by J-bolts and the metal plate apparatus. But the big bang slab had no place to insert J-bolts. In fact, it was almost crackless. Any breeze could shove the tower off. The girders had to be secured to it, but how?

At the end of the boulder nearest the wall was a single crevice wide enough for a bag's worth of ready-mix and a J-bolt. One anchor against a cosmos of storms.

On the ocean side, the boulder subsided into the earth and gave way to big rocks, firmly embedded beneath the hardscrabble. Between these rocks I sank a few more bags of cement mix and rebar reinforcements with J-bolts and plates to hold the ends of the girders, which I allowed to jut out a few feet from the boulder.

I was now anchored in three places. Four anchors would have been better, and five or six better still. It wasn't perfect, but that's all the boulder offered me.

I worried. And kept on keeping on.

The boulder was incredibly flat for a rock, but not absolutely so. The level indicated that the southern girder was low by just over an inch on the wall end. I blocked it up with a shim, a piece of scrap wood lying flat. The lumberyard was happy to get rid of such scraps for free. I nailed this shim through its side up into the girder, which was now level but seemed a bit tentative to me—an entire corner of the tower would rest on that brief chunk. I worried, but took hope in the fact that I'd seen many Maine barns supported by such shims and they had survived decades of winters.

So what if the shim shimmied out? If a raccoon required it, or the earth shrugged? The tower might tilt a little, but then so did Pisa's tower and the Torre degli Asinelli. If it leaned and didn't shatter on the wall, I'd charge admission. The Leaning Tower of Sedgwick.

I worried and soldiered on.

I placed the joists on edge, centered on marks every 16 inches. After checking them for level and shimming them with shingles if required, I toenailed them into the girders with 16d (3½") galvanized nails, two nails on one side of the joist, one on the other. I could have used the longer and thicker 20d nails, but they usually split the wood so badly that it wasn't worth it. These 16d's were hefty enough, and they'd have to be—they would hold the whole works down as the wind tried to lift, shift, and flatten it.

I also added sections of bridging between the joists at the girders to decrease wobble. At this point I could have installed two-inch solid Styrofoam insulation between the joists. The Styrofoam comes in 4' × 8' sheets, cuts easily with a knife, and could have been laid just under the future floor in rows supported by lath or nailheads, snugged up between the joists. But since this was a summertime tower, I decided against it.

With the joists in place, the CDX (exterior grade) plywood flooring (rough on the down side, smooth on the up) was next—4' × 8' sheets, ½ inch thick. For a stronger, bounce-free floor, or if you are thinking of installing a heavy woodstove or grand piano in your tower, I'd suggest ⅝-inch plywood.

I could also have used a cheaper product called chipboard in Maine—nasty-looking stuff contrived out of wood chips and glue, about 90 percent glue, I suspect. Chipboard might have been okay if I'd planned to cover it with a pine plank or hardwood floor. But pine and hardwood were expensive. Besides, plywood is the unofficial state floor of Maine.

I nailed my plywood to the joists every foot or so with 8d galvanized nails. Later, I planned to paint it, or cover it with a fancy rug from the East Hampton dump. The beach crowd there was always tiring of and tossing out expensive rugs, sometimes, it seemed, before they had walked on them.

My foundation platform was now complete. I wasn't happy about being attached to my boulder at only three points (I later learned that local stone workers could have drilled into the rock and connected me more securely), and I was anxious about the performance of that key shim, but in more buoyant moments, I congratulated myself on one of the mightiest foundations ever. That rock hadn't moved since the last ice age. And no more ice ages seemed imminent. In fact, just the opposite was coming, some said.

One Sunday afternoon just before I was due to head back to Long Island, I had visitors. Jim and Josephine Adams from Deer Isle walked out of the fog with their two children, Jacob, five, and Esther, two, to inspect my fabled project.

I had met the Adams family while hammering up my cottage there. Once a summer we got together for Josephine's homemade pizza. For the rest of the summer we waved to each other while passing in our cars. They lived down one of the mysterious dirt roads that wander off into the woods all over Deer Isle and

Sedgwick. Some roads go back for miles and seem to hold deep secrets. Many lead to one-room cabins fashioned by 1960s dropouts, or by followers of Helen and Scott Nearing, who lived in Harborside on the edge of the Penobscot. Scott died a few years ago, at age one hundred, but Helen, in her eighties, carried on alone for a while, proving that, as she put it, "a lone woman can live productively, fend for herself, gardening and wood-toting and housekeeping and living in nature with a sense of fulfillment and purpose." Their book, *The Good Life*, remains a bible of the back-to-the-land movement.

Jim Adams moved here after graduating from the University of Michigan in the 1970s, not in thrall to the Nearings but because he had heard of Down East Maine's reputation as a beautiful place with cheap land and real jobs you could do with your hands and feel good about. He met Josephine, an immigrant from Pennsylvania, at a contra dance in Blue Hill and built her a 15' × 20' cabin, where they lived until Jacob was born. Then they moved into a proper two-story clapboard Jim constructed right next to the cabin.

"What do you think you are doing?" Jim asked point-blank. As a fellow builder, he was allowed to put questions like that, no diplomacy required.

"Building a tower," I said nervously. A professional was gazing at my foundation.

"Like Ulysses," he nodded.

Who's that? I wondered. Another local tower guy? On this hill? I didn't get it, and let it pass to talk to the kids, who were attempting to stir Opie into a round of rock chasing. Opie was having none of it. "Beagles don't do that," I explained. Instead Opie rolled over and the kids scratched his ample belly. Opie needed to go on a diet.

Jim and Josephine, like just about everybody around here, worked at many jobs. Jim did some weekend lobster fishing and on weekdays labored at a friend's construction company. He also played bass fiddle for the Bangor Symphony and trained every evening after work for various long-distance-running events. The previous year he had finished third in the Stonington Fourth of July 10-kilometer race. His goal was the annual Portland marathon. Josephine was a house painter, a Sheetrocker, a deacon at the Stonington Episcopal Church, and the kids' caretaker.

Jim kept staring at my work.

"Whadya think?" I asked.

"It depends on what you're going to put on it. So far, so good."

I noticed a mosquito on Jim's cheek and pointed it out. Jim ignored my warning. He was of the local school that refused to be bothered by bugs. Only people from "away" let bugs bother them.

As they went back into the fog with the kids, Jim invited me to the Bangor Symphony's next concert in Ellsworth—Copland, Beethoven, Shostakovich. I said I'd try to make it.

He said no more about my tower idea. In Maine you were allowed to go crazy as you wished.

Jim's remark about Ulysses stayed with me until, in the middle of the night, I got the dry joke. Ulysses was a reference to James Joyce's novel, not some fellow tower-dreamer. There was a tower at the start of the book, perhaps a dim influence on my subconscious. I hadn't read *Ulysses* for perhaps twenty years and, to tell the truth, had yet to finish it, a work in progress. After I drove back to East Hampton at the end of June, I uncovered much about that tower, including Joyce's lines that Jim referred to— page 1, first sentence. It's 8 a.m., June 16, 1904.

Stately, plump Buck Milligan came from the stairhead, bearing a bowl of lather on which a mirror and a razor lay crossed. A yellow dressing-gown, ungirdled, was sustained gently behind him by the mild morning air. He held the bowl aloft and intoned:

— *Introibo ad altare Dei.*

Halted, he peered down the dark winding stairs and called up coarsely:

— Come up, Kinch. Come up, you fearful jesuit.

Solemnly he came forward and mounted the round gunrest. He faced about and blessed gravely thrice the tower, the surrounding country and the awaking mountains.

The academics differ on their interpretations of Joyce's tower. Some say Stephen Dedalus abandoned the tower he shared with Buck Mulligan as a symbol of Joyce's "forsaking of Celtic romanticism." Whatever the spin, the tower is real: Martello Tower Number 11 can be found at Sandycove, Dublin, in fine repair.

Martellos were among the most prevalent single-design towers in the world. They were also the ugliest—squat, thick of wall, gun-topped, soldier-

Joyce's tower [*CORBIS/Michael St. Maur Sheil*]

garrisoned at midheight, and bottomed out with a store of explosives.

More than one hundred Martello towers were piled up at great expense and in haste, most of them from 1803 to 1815, to defend the English and Irish coasts against Napoleon's threatened sea invasion. Later, many were raised in North America, from Key West to Montreal to Halifax. Ironically, they were all named and modeled on a French tower in Corsica that had resisted English attack.

Even more ironically, none of them ever fired a shot in defense. England's best and brightest military minds erected heaps of useless eyesores. The dozens that still stand have been converted into houses, cafés, and amusement parks. All the others have fallen victim to the sea, to vandals, or to brambles.

The actual Martello that Joyce described had been rented from the War Office in 1904 for eight pounds so that Joyce's friend, Oliver St. John Gogarty, might write a novel there. Joyce stayed in the Martello only a few days before a clash of temperaments drove him to seek shelter elsewhere. But something about that tower touched him; maybe its lonely ugliness, or its futility.

If you want to build such a tower in honor of *Ulysses*, or perhaps, like Gogarty, to write a novel in, you should note the following details: Martellos were made of brick or stone on a foundation of the same. Usually, but not always, Martellos were surfaced with stucco to provide a slick surface for cannonballs and bullets to skip off of. Walls were at least eight feet thick on the side of expected attack, usually the ocean side. Martellos were round, from twenty-four to forty feet high, with a base diameter of thirty-five to forty feet, slightly less at the peak.

Most important, if you are being a purist about your Martello imitation, your door must be at least ten feet off the ground on the second floor and accessible only by a ladder that can be withdrawn if an enemy (nosy neighbor, book critic, etc.) shows up. This arrival of an enemy is an event that all surviving Martellos still anticipate.

If you intend to reside in your Martello, like Joyce and Gogarty, prepare for constant dampness and darkness—only two minuscule windows are permitted on the second-floor garrison level. You will not be distracted from composing your novel by gazing out your window. Also, use no metal other than copper, since other metals produce sparks easily and your entire magazine (as in gunpowder) on the first floor might go off with you and your novel.

Your roof, built of wood or arched brick, will be surrounded by a six-foot parapet. Your main gun, if you choose to be armed, will be mounted on a raised section at the center of the roof. This is your traversing gun. You might also provide a few howitzers and a carronade.

These Martellos remind me of our nuclear missile silos—our inverted towers—in their total devotion to slaughter, their unspeakable gracelessness, and the fact that they have—so far—never been used as intended and paid for.

William Cobbett, a radical journalist and acute observer of the British military, checked out the Martellos on the Kent coast in 1823 and filed the following report:

> Here has been the squandering! Here has been the pauper-making! . . . To think that I should be destined to behold these monuments of Pitt! . . . Here they are, piles of bricks in circular form . . . Cannons were to be fired from the top of these things, in order to defend the country from the French Jacobins! I think I counted along here upwards of thirty of these ridiculous things, which I daresay cost five, perhaps ten thousand pounds each . . . I daresay they cost millions.

Martello tower (section detail) [*Lauren Jarrett*]

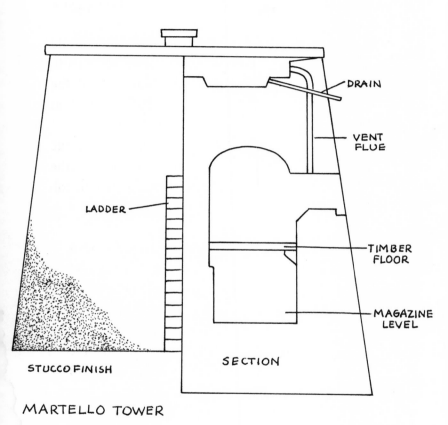

DRAIN

VENT
FLUE

LADDER

TIMBER
FLOOR

MAGAZINE
LEVEL

STUCCO FINISH

SECTION

MARTELLO TOWER

James Joyce offered literary immortality to one of these sorry stacks. Perhaps our times will find an author to do the same for missile silos; maybe someday they too will be amusement parks, cafés, and shelters for writers.

RAGE

Up to this moment little had been required of me physically beyond the hard hauling of supplies, the anchoring of girders, and the hammering of level joists. Now it was time to climb nearer to vertigo territory.

At this point I was thankful I hadn't dragged a generator into the woods and hooked up a power saw or power anything. Out of nowhere, and for the first time in my fifty-four years, I had fallen into a consuming anger. The cause was a cliché: my wife had forgotten my birthday. Then, I imagined she had developed an interest in another man, and recently she had barraged me with general complaints, my tower fascination among them. I spent nights on the East Hampton living room couch trying to break out of my anger into love. "Break out, break out, break out," I commanded. But the rage would not stop.

I suspected Annie felt the same. I imagined she wanted me gone. The woman I adored, who had borne my daughter, who slept beside me for over seventeen years, was now, I fantasized, my potential assassin. My foundations of home and faith were evaporating in a marital fury.

Holly remained, but I couldn't share any of this with her. My maelstrom would terrify her and so would my tremendous need for her. Talking to her was complicated, in any case: against my vehement protests, on the last day of school, Annie had taken Holly to England to visit her sister for a few weeks.

I was, in short, hysterical.

And alone again in the Maine woods without power tools.

As Thomas Merton observed, tough, common work—chores—is a great purifier. Such chores saved me. Hand-sawing those studs, slamming in those 16d's, hefting frames into place on the platform with nobody around to help me if I lost my footing and the frame toppled back on me, concentrated my rage and dissipated my hysteria. If chores did not bring me peace, at least they left me exhausted and relatively passive at the end of each day.

Towers have been built for many reasons, as the various appreciations in this book demonstrate. Mine, conceived in emptiness when my memoir was finished, was founded on the edge of despair and framed in pure frenzy, a dark rage in bright sunlight. If I believed in demons, I would credit them for all the first-floor frames. I was so far from love then that I didn't know how to get back, or what I was trying to get back to.

Later I discovered that an astonishing series of modern towers had been created by a man who, in a similar mood, happened to share some of my demons.

When I started my project, I associated the Watts Towers with the 1965 race riots in Los Angeles, California. I assumed they were piles of debris somehow fashioned as a memorial to those who had died in the riots.

I needed an education.

The Watts Towers, as nearly everybody else knows, were the creations of Simon Rodia, a bad-tempered, lyrical little guy with enormous energy. Rodia, or

"Sam" as he was later known, was born in a village near Naples, Italy, that annually celebrated a pageant dating from the Middle Ages and featuring great ceremonial towers—eight of them, six stories high and weighing three tons each.

Sam Rodia left Italy at age fifteen and wandered here and there around the United States until he was hired in California as a cement worker. As his third marriage failed in 1921, he started his first tower, and he didn't quit until 1955, when he had completed three lacy, intricately decorated spirals of wire and reinforced concrete in his backyard—the Watts Towers. Two of these towers are almost one hundred feet tall and the third a mere fifty-five feet.

Why did he do it? Nobody knows. Some say he was nostalgically duplicating those ceremonial towers of his boyhood village. My friend the poet Marvin Bell tells me it's obvious: "They're masts on an imaginary boat, a boat to sail home in."

Whatever Sam intended, his towers are like no other towers on earth and of no rational value whatsoever—they host no radio or TV beacons, no viewing platform, no elevators or stairs, not even a ladder to ascend. They were devised in a combination of

The Watts Towers [*CORBIS/G. E. Kidder Smith*]

playfulness, crankiness, and many unknowns and executed over decades with ritual determination by an amateur visionary who used only the most basic tools. He didn't even bother with a scaffold.

Sam's backyard was the tip of his triangular one-tenth-of-an-acre lot on a dead-end street in the Watts section of Los Angeles. In the 1920s and '30s Watts was a working-class area buffeted by dust and dirt blown from every direction. Southern Pacific freight trains roared by Sam's house four times a day; plus there was the continual racket of Pacific Electric streetcars, the two major transit lines of the Big Red Cars, and five others running to and from Long Beach, Redondo Beach, and elsewhere, carrying a weekly total of 75,000 passengers. It was like living at the center of JFK, O'Hare, or LAX airport.

When Sam moved into his tiny house on his minuscule patch, he was married to his third wife, Carmen (he had three children from a previous marriage). Soon the noise, the traffic, and Sam's obsessive building drove Carmen away. He was alone at forty-two, determined never to marry again. And free.

Sam didn't bother to ask the local authorities for a tower permit—he couldn't have, in any case, since he had no formal plans. He made it all up as he went along and paid for his materials out of what was left from his small salary.

Sam's foundations were no more than a foot and a half deep, about as illegal as you can get. Los Angeles code stipulated a twenty-four-foot depth for buildings one hundred feet high.

Using no bolts, rivets, or welds, Sam bent scrap metal into any shape he desired, wrapped it with whatever wire he had handy, and fastened it all together with his special cement recipe. As levels of the tower's cement hardened, he used them to continue his ascent.

He explained: "I did it all myself. I never had a single help. I don't have no money. Another thing, if I hired a man, he don't know what to do. A million times, I don't know what to do myself."

Working after his day job and on weekends, this small man, attached only by a safety harness, scrambled up his spires, hauling buckets of cement and constructions that were embedded with cast-off decorations: 11,000 pieces of broken pottery, 15,000 glazed tiles, 6,000 glass bottle chips, dozens of mirrors, 10,000 seashells, hundreds of rocks, chunks of marble, and slices of linoleum.

To strengthen his creations, he used whatever turned up in the dump or on the street: a corrugated water pipe, a bike wheel, railroad ties and spikes, water buckets, airplane wing supports, pots, pans, colanders, even a bowling ball.

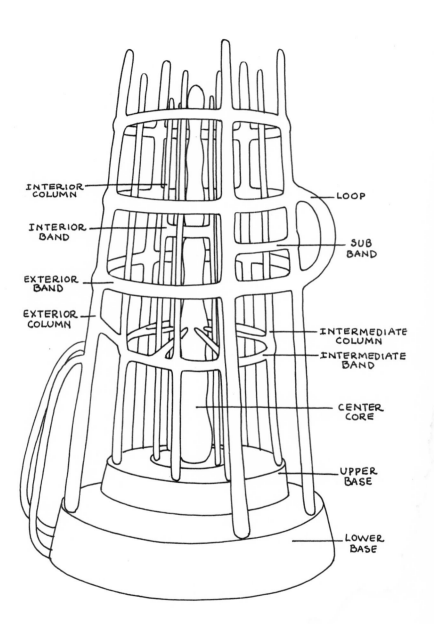

INTERIOR COLUMN

INTERIOR BAND

EXTERIOR BAND

EXTERIOR COLUMN

LOOP

SUB BAND

INTERMEDIATE COLUMN

INTERMEDIATE BAND

CENTER CORE

UPPER BASE

LOWER BASE

Sam Rodia was one of the world's great eccentrics and, like Eiffel, he got mixed reviews. His wives said he was impossible; relatives called him a drunk (a Watts neighbor, the jazz legend Charles Mingus, recalled him more fondly, admitting that "Sam liked a glass of good red wine"). Others branded him an anarchist because he was always angry about the police, the government, the Catholic Church, and academics for their treatment of his heroes, Marco Polo and Christopher Columbus. Sam detested immigration authorities—out of spite, he lied about his age and exit date from Italy on his official papers. Journalists got no better from him. When asked by reporters to explain his towers, he offered: "I buried my wife under them," "I lost my job!" or (perhaps more to the point) "I just wanted to do something big."

When interrogated by inspectors from the Los Angeles Building and Safety Department in 1948, he mocked them: "I build the towers in honor of the highways of California. I build that tower 101 feet tall in honor of Highway 101. I build that tower 99 feet tall in honor of Highway 99. I build that tower 66 feet tall in honor of Highway 66."

A Watts tower (section detail) [*Lauren Jarrett*]

The inspectors were not amused. A decade later their department declared that the towers must come down. They scheduled a stress test and tried to yank one over. The crane broke. The tower stood.

Finally, they retreated in the face of a gathering storm of international outrage, and comments like these:

> The work of Simon Rodia's hands [is] a monument in the twentieth century to take us back to the simple, happy, fundamental skill from which our knowledge of the laws of mechanics grows. (Jacob Bronowski, *The Ascent of Man*)

> Sam came in with what today would be called ferro-cement structure. He thought in terms of very thin shells with a great deal of wire mesh deeply imbedded in it . . . I believe in [his] intuitive intelligence and the dynamics of genius . . . Almost all great design is first intuitive design. (R. Buckminster Fuller)

Sam Rodia left his towers in 1955 at age seventy-six, too old to continue with his art. Hailed as an innocent Antonio Gaudí, he died ten years later in Northern California, celebrated at last for his furious tenacity. The Watts Towers are now a State Historic Park.

To me, his soaring spires are the ultimate in back-yard tower construction—dances of caprice, anger, joy, and nostalgia.

Incidentally, his towers have withstood seven major earthquakes. They are also the tallest structures ever made by one man alone.

STUD

If you build all day, every day, as I did for many summertime weeks, you will emerge a far younger man; if not a stud, at least a thinner, well-muscled older guy. Your body shows you what it can still do, what it has saved for you. You learn to trust it all over again, the way you once did as a playground kid.

Also comforting was Annie and Holly's safe return from England to Maine. Holly now honed her canoeing and sailing skills at a nearby camp on a large lake called, in typical Maine understatement, Walker Pond, while her dad pursued his tower passion.

Annie said she had missed me in England. Every lunch hour she drove to Christy Hill and delivered a homemade sandwich for "Builder Bill." She makes a terrific sandwich.

The 2" × 4" × 8' kiln-dried fir stud is the basic item of wood tower construction. The studs are dubbed 2 × 4's, but that's their untrimmed measurement. Actually, they are 1½" × 3½" and a bit more than eight feet long. Why they aren't tagged as such I don't know. Tradition from their untrimmed days, I guess. Plus, "1½" × 3½"" takes longer to say. Whatever they are called, these studs were the uprights that framed the tower's four walls at each level.

Framing a plain Quaker tower like mine was simple. Using my platform as a staging area, and starting at the southern side, I placed an 11-foot-5-inch 2 × 4 on its 2-inch side. That was the bottom sill, also named the soleplate, the portion of the wall that was to be nailed into the deck later.

Now, with a pencil I marked the sill every 16 inches. (A pencil is the preferred marking tool; often I worked in the rain, and a ballpoint pen won't mark on wet wood.) Centered on these marks I would later nail the studs. It was important to place the studs precisely on the center of their marks, especially at the four- and eight-foot spots—the sheathing of four-foot-wide plywood panels would meet at the center of these key studs.

On the south side I framed out a rough opening for a door. It was tempting to add a few windows here also, but since this was the bottom portion of the tower, I limited my downstairs window plans. Down here I was building for strength. A mostly uninterrupted wall is stronger than one broken by lots of openings, as traditional tower builders knew.

Many ancient towers were fitted with only one door, often placed at an inconvenient height. The most renowned of these are the mysterious Irish Round Towers, which have survived in Ireland for over one thousand years.

In each of the Irish Round Towers, the thick wooden door is high off the ground. Since the towers always stand among the ruins of monasteries, they were probably passive defensive bastions for the monks who, upon spotting a Viking raiding party, gathered all the monastery's manuscripts and sacred objects and climbed into the tower, pulling up the entrance ladder after them and clambering from floor to floor, hauling up ladders as they ascended. That's how the Irish monks saved Western civilization from the Norse worshipers of Odin.

Seventy-eight of these towers still survive and twenty are totally intact. They were well built of stone with wooden floors and one tiny window per floor, and ranged in height from 60 to 130 feet and from 13 to 19 feet in diameter, slightly smaller at the top.

There's not a shred of decoration on any Irish Round Tower, which makes it more likely that they were purely defensive and not, as some speculate, fire temples, druid shrines, astronomical observatories, altars to Baal, beacons, stylite columns, or phallic emblems thrown up by a variety of people, among them the Carthaginians, the Danes, and the Phoenicians.

Since I expected no invaders (Maine is usually listed as the most crime-free state in the nation), I framed my door's rough opening at ground level. My door, from the East Hampton dump, was a handsome red exterior wooden door with three amusing peep windows. I marked the door's width on the bottom sill for the jack studs there, leaving a half inch extra for the door to swing. Since the door was 6' 5" high, I nailed 6' 5½" jack studs next to the marks on each side of the bottom sill. To each jack stud, and also through the sill, I nailed a standard eight-foot stud with 16d's.

At the top of the jack studs, I placed my door header, two planks of 2" × 8" fir, nailed into each other and to the 8-foot studs. The jack studs sat under the

header, like a jack, and the header in turn supported all that would be above it.

Finally, I positioned the top plate over the studs. Previously this plate had been marked every 16 inches by placing it next to the bottom sill and aligning the marks precisely. Straight-up vertical studs would be the result. I nailed the top plate to the studs with 16d's as I had done on the bottom sill.

I now had one 11' 5" wall frame ready to raise.

At this point, I considered two schools of sheathing: one says you sheathe on the platform, the other that you sheathe after the frame is raised. If you have friends who can help you lift the weighty sheathed frame, you might opt to sheathe it on the platform, making sure that the frame is straight first. Working alone, I had to sheathe the frame after raising it.

Lifting sheathed or unsheathed frames into place can be a tricky maneuver. Don't try it in a wind, and always have an escape hatch area in case it falls back on you. The first frame I raised at the Deer Isle cottage—a ten-footer with 2" × 6" studs—slipped and slammed back down on top of me. I had planned no escape route. Luckily I was standing near a rough window opening. The frame fell around me and I got

Irish Round Tower [*Robert Welch, CORBIS/Sean Sexton Collection*]

off with shoulder bruises rather than being knocked out or worse.

A 2" × 4" stud frame is not impossibly heavy, but it is clumsy to raise. You are attempting to hold the whole thing upright with one hand and nail through the bottom sill with the other. It helps to have a temporary brace handy or a rope tied at the top of the frame to attach to a nearby tree as a safety lash before you nail through the bottom sill into the platform. After the first frame is raised, the others are much easier to support, as you can tie them or nail them temporarily to the standing frame.

At the end of the east and west wall frames, I tripled the studs, three studs nailed into the sills and plates and to each other. The east and west frames, extending the entire ten-foot width of the deck, butted up against the north and south walls, which were 11' 5" long, and fitted inside them, nailed to the tripled corner studs. When gales blew in from the mountains and ocean, these walls would press in on the north and south walls and be partially supported by them.

Each window required the same jack stud and header assemblage as the door. The headers spanned the space over the windows, and since they would bear much of the weight of the upper floors, the headers and jacks had to be done right. Rough openings for the slider halves were framed into the east and west ends, looking out over ocean and mountains.

When I had constructed and erected all four unsheathed frames—the two 11' 5" frames on the north and south sides, and on either side of them the 10' east and west frames, all nailed with 16d nails into each other and the deck—I was ready for the cat plates. The cat plate is a 2 × 4 on its wide side running over the tops of all the frames, clawing the ends together like a cat's paw. The cat plate on the north and south frames clawed into the ends of the east and west frames.

Sheathing was next. A strong sheathing is almost as important as a secure foundation. I would have preferred pine or spruce plank sheathing, but it was more expensive and not as strong as other sheathings. I also considered T-1-11, for Texture 1-11. These 4' × 8' sheets combine a plywood backing with a textured siding that resembles real boards, if you don't inspect them too closely. Builders use T-1-11 a lot on garages and industrial structures and now and then on houses. But, seeming to be what it is not, it smacks of the fake to me.

I finally picked sheathing of ½-inch CDX plywood with the smooth side facing the interior, to be painted, Sheetrocked, or paneled as I chose. Using protruding

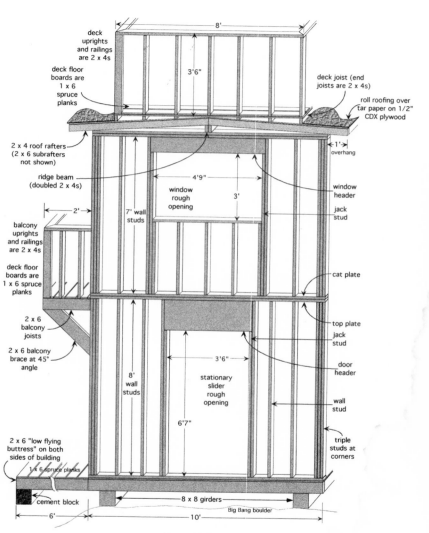

deck uprights and railings are 2 x 4s

deck floor boards are 1 x 6 spruce planks

deck joist (end joists are 2 x 4s)

roll roofing over tar paper on 1/2" CDX plywood

8'

3'6"

2 x 4 roof rafters (2 x 6 subrafters not shown)

1' overhang

ridge beam (doubled 2 x 4s)

window rough opening

4'9"

3'

window header

jack stud

2'

7' wall studs

balcony uprights and railings are 2 x 4s

deck floor boards are 1 x 6 spruce planks

2 x 6 balcony joists

2 x 6 balcony brace at 45° angle

cat plate

top plate

jack stud

door header

3'6"

stationary slider rough opening

8' wall studs

6'7"

wall stud

triple studs at corners

2 x 6 "low flying buttress" on both sides of building

1 x 6 spruce planks

cement block

8 x 8 girders

Big Bang boulder

6'

10'

Frame Detail
East and West Sides

nailheads as a temporary support along the bottom sill, I nailed the plywood about every foot to the upright frames with 8d nails, covering the frames completely except at the rough door and window openings.

With all four frames sheathed, I was ready to think about the next floor and a serious venture into vertigo.

I sat on my cat plate, feet firmly resting on the ladder, and caught myself feeling rather proud about all of this so far. During casual tower research at the Blue Hill Library in the evening, I had uncovered some reminders about such pride, and more on the dark side of towers. I was reminded that Bannadonna, the arrogant Italian engineer in Melville's "The Bell Tower," erected a high tower to house a bell-ringing mechanism that eventually killed him.

Edgar Allan Poe's poem "The City in the Sea" visited the city of Gomorrah, drowned in the Dead Sea for its sins:

> *While from a proud tower in the town*
> *Death looks gigantically down.*

Christy Hill tower (framing detail) [*Steve Taylor*]

In Ibsen's play *The Master Builder*, the tower was another symbol of arrogance, and its builder, who, like me, suffered from acrophobia, succumbed because of overconfidence. Inspired by a charming lady, he scaled his creation to place a wreath at the top and, in a whirl of vertigo, lost his balance and toppled to his death.

I recalled my parents upbraiding me for hubris: "Who do you think you are?" they demanded after one of my teen rants against the church. I'd better watch it. I allowed myself a half glass of wine against vertigo.

Above me the first of the August Perseid showers decorated the twilight. I was feeling boyish, with the exception of that constant twinge down where I thought my liver might be. It twinged, subsided, twinged again and would not stop. I tried to forget it by concentrating on the shooting stars.

Perhaps liver payment was now due for decades of appreciation of "a glass of good red wine," as Charles Mingus delicately put it.

HARVEST

When I was a fresh adolescent, suddenly aware that God might not be the scary thunderbolt fellow I'd heard about in church, I used to open my bedroom window and reach out my hand to him in the night sky. He was up there somewhere. He would let me know who he was. And if I held my hand out the window to him long enough, someday he would reach past the stars and touch my fingers.

Now, as a late-middle-aged tower builder, I still needed a God like that, a fellow who came down and fixed stuff like diseases, rages, and vertigoes. But I still had no idea how to deal with such a God or dare to pray to him. My current god ideas of Oceanic Love, Universal Spirit, and Primal Source didn't have an immediate bedside manner. I longed for practical help from the sky, and this August, the sky wouldn't even rain on us. The *Ellsworth American* newspaper warned that forest-fire danger was extreme and the blueberry harvest would be a disaster without a storm soon. We needed a God of deluge.

As I built the tower's second floor, the blueberry bosses began their preparations in the fields below me. The crew leaders portioned off wide paths with string for the local and migrant workers who would arrive soon and, bent over in the sun, gather berries all day with their aluminum rakes. The fields were hot, about ten degrees warmer than my woods, and infested with bees nesting underground and stinging often. It was nasty work, but a raker could earn two thousand dollars in a few weeks for the Maine harvest.

The loudspeaker voices of the crew chiefs bounced off the hills as they organized the sections. A winnowing machine, to clean the berries of leaves and stems, stood hopefully at the center of the fields surrounded by stacks of blue plastic tubs that the rakers would fill with berries, shriveled or plump, depending on next week's weather. Since fields were harvested only every two years, each cloud formation was studied for promise of moisture.

I, too, was dry. The liver twinges had started in the spring, after a week of back-to-back parties and dinners. I had ignored them at first. Muscle cramps, a bum appendix, cancer? Or nothing. I was rarely sick and I didn't even know a handy doctor. Just to be safe, I diagnosed myself with liver exhaustion. After thirty years of evening indulgence and occasional weekend overindulgence, I quit booze cold turkey. The glass that had urged a timid man to loquaciousness, that had often spurred a dull brain to inspiration (and often to even deeper dullness), was empty.

For a while I felt charged with a new energy and was wonderfully clearheaded, the brief pink cloud that recovering alcoholics report. The pains diminished but didn't stop. Was it my turn to get sick now? The solace of a glass of red was gone. Only now and then did I dare a sip, and that sip now brought on more anxiety about the state of my liver than calm.

But I monkeyed up the ladder and nailed the next nail and monkeyed down and sawed and nailed, and the constant motion, not booze, became the balm that drove me from fear to fear.

For the next floor, I decided to use seven-foot wall studs, not the usual eight-footers—less height but also less to wobble in the wind, I guessed. Also, the second floor's joists would be fixed inside the first floor's cat plates. I intuited that this would bind the tower together as one unit while slightly reducing the mass available for the wind to play with. Intuitive Engineering, I named it.

The do-it-yourself home improvement manuals disagreed with Intuitive Engineering. Most experts required that the second floors of a building be constructed with 2" × 6" joists (or 2" × 8" for longer spans) that were toenailed on top of the cat plates, just as the first-floor joists were toenailed on top of the two girders.

My Intuitive Engineering suggested the contrary: wind wobble would decrease if the joists hung from the joist hangers that were nailed to the inside of the cat and top plates, one hanger for each end of the joist on 16-inch centers.

The joist hanger is a most unlikely apparatus. It scoops up the end of the joist with about an inch and a half of metal. The hanger is nailed to the joist and the rest of it is fastened to the cat plate and top plate with 8d nails on each side of the hanger. The joist hanger doesn't look strong enough to hang a winter coat on, but it works. You can jump up and down on the joist all you like without dislodging it or bending the hanger.

Intuitive Engineering dictated that the joists be placed so that their top sides were flush with the surface of the cat plates. Then it was just a repeat of making the first-floor platform.

I hauled up 4' × 8' sheets of ½-inch CDX plywood by lassoing the sheets at midpoint, yanking the noose tight, shouting "It's show time!" to the universe, and, after a deep breath, dragging them upward.

At the second floor, the plywood was nailed into the cat plates and each joist, a nail about every foot. The result: a flat floor, just like the platform below, ready to receive 2" × 4" × 7' studs on bottom sills, capped by top and cat plates. There would be rough openings for the east and west side-by-side windows — each slightly more than 3 feet high and 4 feet 9 inches wide. With two hinged windows on each end, the upstairs would dance in constant light.

For the heck of it and without a plan, I framed in a rough opening for a wooden closet door I had uncovered in the Deer Isle dump. Since Maine people don't throw much away (they fix it or store it), this perfect little door was a real find.

Perhaps outside stairs would proceed up to the closet door, I briefly imagined. No, they wouldn't—outside stairs allowed marauders access to the peak. Any tower worth its name incorporated an inside stairway.

Well then, the little door would lead to a balcony perhaps. Plenty of balconies on towers—Pisa and Babel, for instance. A balcony to pour liquids on marauders, or sing a song in the moonlight. A song to Annie, perhaps. She always accused me of being as romantic as a toad. Maybe a moonlight balcony serenade would help my image with her.

Then I saw it—that balcony would square up my ten-by-twelve-foot box by adding two feet on the shorter side. At last I had a traditional square tower—twelve by twelve feet.

I framed out the balcony with two pressure-treated horizontal 2" × 6" joists that were in turn supported by 2" × 6" braces on a 45-degree angle back to the first floor, nailed into the studs and sheathing on either side of the main door's rough opening. Across the balcony joists, I nailed 1" × 6" × 3' spruce planks, treated later with a clear waterproofing. On top of the planks, 2" × 4" uprights and railings completed the closet door/balcony frolic.

The sheathing of the second floor was similar to that of the first floor except that I sheathed the top portion of each frame with 2' × 8' half-panels before I lifted it, and sheathed the bottom portion from my ladder after the frame was upright. This partial sheathing added to the weight of the frame, but it was not too much of a chore to lift it. After the frame was in place and nailed to the deck and cat-pawed to its sister frames, I didn't have to worry about dragging heavy and clumsy full 4' × 8' plywood panels up the ladder alone—a tricky, dangerous job.

Near the end of August, I stood on my roofless second floor and peered into the twilight through my huge rough window openings to both sea and mountains, hoping to see a final shooting star. But the Perseid showers were done for this summer.

Straight up, a bald eagle nonchalantly suffered the attacks of two indistinct lesser birds that it had somehow offended. Tiring of them, the eagle dove in a sort of roll toward me, its immense wings churning down a wall of rushing air.

A mass of weighty clouds poured over the western mountains, for a time promising rain, but delivering only a spectacular sundown of pale Maine yellow and thunderous black. Below the sunset the stacked blue buckets waited in the string-lined fields.

Somewhere over that horizon in New York and Chicago, advance reviews of my memoir were being printed in book trade publications. But from up here, you couldn't see a review.

Hints of grace were here, tumults of gratitude that knocked me suddenly to my knees in thanksgiving to a nameless, unnameable something. For what? For this, for all of it. To witness those clouds and mountains, that sun, the eagle, to have been granted more than fifty years to do just this. I was no longer a writer or publisher or any other definable entity. I was free from words, and bowed down by simple thanks.

PETRIFIED

It was time for the acrophobe to confront his topple-forward vertigo. I could construct most of the roof supports from the floor below, but to complete the roofing I would have to climb up on top of the tower.

The roof was to be my third floor. Next summer I might dare to go higher. But for now it would be the dreaming deck, and it would also have to slope slightly to shed rains and be strong enough to support gargantuan winter snows. In short, sloping, but not so sloping as to be un-walkable, and mighty, but not so weighty that the tower was top-heavy.

Since there were no blueprints, I took the advice of Intuitive Engineering at crucial moments. From here on up all my stress points were imagined. I examined, held, and ran my hand over boards to figure out what they might support in snow, in people.

One of the most eloquent tributes to Intuitive Engineering is Carol Shields' novel *The Stone Diaries*. Her hero, Cuyler Goodwill, who has just lost his young wife, stands by her grave in Manitoba and realizes that the grave marker is "pitifully inadequate, too meagre and insubstantial for the creature who had been his sweetheart, his wife, his treasure." Little by little, he starts to construct a stone tower to her memory. "He chooses the stones carefully, for he had formed an odd resolution, which is that he will set them without mortar. Gravity alone must hold them in place, gravity and balance, each stone receptive to the shape of those it rests against and in keeping with the abstraction that has late filled his head like a walking reverie, a dream structure made up of sorrow mingled with bewilderment."

Eventually Goodwill's tower, assembled from stones no bigger than a thumb or fist, and others ten inches across, rises to thirty feet, hollow at the core, around his wife's grave.

When I read Shields' novel, I wondered again about my "tower for no reason." Was it really, at least in part, a monument to my baby child? Was this passion really just an attempt to stop time and hold it against the sea and sky?

There wasn't much leisure for hunkered-down pondering of intangibles on that hill. The tower's roof had to be completed soon. Holly's camp on Walker Pond just over the next ridge was in its final days. Annie, Holly, Opie, and I had to return to Long Island for Holly's entrance into sixth grade. Already some maples were turning red and gold. The bugs were gone. Evenings had a nip.

In a typical gable-end construction, the side walls, not the gable-end walls, take most of the roof's weight. But for this tower, I imagined all four walls would help carry the roof.

Planning only a slight pitch, I nailed together two fourteen-foot-long 2 × 4's and toenailed them as a ridge beam from one gable end to the other—from sea to mountain side—and a foot out over the edge on each side. The gables, if they could be called that with such a minimal pitch, were thus only 3½ inches higher at the peak (the thickness of the 2 × 4) than at the sides.

Under the double 2" × 4" beam and snug against it, I positioned three 2" × 6" sub-rafters at equal intervals, suspended from joist hangers on the north and south walls. These sub-rafters seemed adequate to carry the ridge beam and the roof's weight, but it was just a guess.

On top of the ridge beam at one-foot intervals, I toenailed (nailed from the side) the ends of the main roof rafters, six-foot-long 2×4's that met end to end on the ridge beam and extended for a foot over the north and south sides to provide eaves.

To help ensure that the roof would not blow off in a gale, I secured the $2" \times 4"$ rafters to the $2" \times 6"$ sub-rafters with foot-wide plywood strips at three equal intervals for each sub-rafter.

At the peak of the roof, slightly to the sea side, I framed out a small hatch, large enough to squeeze through after climbing a simple, rough ladder built of two ten-foot 2×4's with $1" \times 6"$ rungs nailed to them. The $2" \times 4"$ rafters on each side of the hatch were doubled up and extra rafters ran to the cat plates from the middle of the hatch base on each side, to offer extra strength when people dragged themselves up through the hatch.

The gathering crisis had arrived. I lassoed my $4' \times 8'$ plywood sheets, hauled them to the second floor through the window openings, and shoved some on top of the rafters. Standing on the top rung of my rough ladder in the hatch opening and reaching out as far as possible, I got a few 8d nails through each sheet into the rafters below, enough to hold them temporarily against the breeze. But in order to nail them, finally, every foot of every rafter, and then to tar-paper and cover my roof with rolled roofing, I would have to get myself up there, something I had not done since I was a tree-house-building kid. If I couldn't manage it, the tower was doomed.

What I needed at this point was a shrink. Carl Gustav Jung, a fellow tower lover, would have been perfect, but he was long dead. He might have understood why a guy who is terrified and dizzied by heights, whose constant nightmare is one of falling from a high place, suffers from a compulsion to climb.

Jung's tower at Bollingen, on Upper Lake Zurich, Switzerland, was started in 1923 and expanded as Jung's insights and moods dictated over the next thirty years. The result was not a single tower but an assemblage of peaks that recalls the Tower of London, which is not a pedigreed tower but a citadel, according to our snooty definition. Jung called his tower his "confession of faith in stone." Like Robinson Jeffers, he did much of the construction himself, working with local Italian masons.

Jung analyzed his fascination as a childhood leftover: "I was passionately fond of playing with bricks, and built towers which I then rapturously destroyed by an 'earthquake.'" He also recognized ancient symbolism in his tower, "a place of religious experience, of

introspection, of astrological investigation, of refuge."
Jung retreated there from the world for months at a
time to engage the mysteries of his psyche, chop wood
for heat and fuel, cook his own food, pump water by
hand, and read by oil lamps.

"In the Tower at Bollingen it is as if one lived in
many centuries simultaneously," Jung wrote. "The place
will outlive me, and in its location and style it points
backward to things of long ago. There is very little about
it to suggest the present . . . There is nothing to disturb
the dead, neither electric light nor telephone."

Maybe Jung would have burrowed into my curious
mind. In addition to my liver twinges, I had developed
a host of chronic hypochondriacal illnesses, among them
an ache in my groin (lymphoma, for sure) and a perpet-
ually clogged right nostril (sinus cancer, no doubt). These
replaced the "cancerous" bump on my chest that a der-
matologist told me would fall off within a week or so,
which it did. My great panic was that Holly would
grow up fatherless, remembering her dad as a dim, weak
figure, as I recalled my own grandparents. Her final
memory of me would be simple: a sick man.

Panic, I read somewhere, is a rather common American problem. We live in a witless electronic era with
little grounding in wisdom or thought, and people eas-

ily lose their way. They freak out. But in my fifty-plus years I had never been touched by panic beyond a single episode of stage fright as a young editor at a Doubleday editorial meeting. I froze, could not even murmur about the book proposal I was presenting to my twenty assembled colleagues. That awful panic was long in my past, I assumed. Until now. Until my friends had cancer. Until I thought I did, too.

This new panic wasn't constant. It had rushed over me briefly in episodes earlier that summer that often gave way to renewed religious ecstasy and terrific bursts of physical energy. I remember in June a 35-mile bike ride to nowhere at reckless speed after a mild panic attack, and later a marathon basketball game with Holly, a version of "horse" that we expanded into a spelling of "antidisestablishment-arianism." Holly won by two letters.

But when panic hit, and I tried to control it ("get a grip," as the usual advice puts it), I found I couldn't, and therefore panicked even more. Then I panicked because I panicked because I panicked, and spun into a free fall that resembled true madness.

In my journal I recorded one of those attacks that summer: "Full panic attack after spat with Annie, dreams that fracture like idiot sound bites, sleep that won't last more than these sound bites, a certainty through the night that I am losing my mind totally—

that a cancer is creeping up my spine to my brain and by dawn I will be raving . . . I can't live another day of panic attacks. This will be my last day if I can't get some control."

Because I was in no shape to drive, Annie chauffeured me to a doctor recommended by a friend. He said I was fine, the liver was a tad spongy, the groin pain was an infected gland, and the clogged nose was just a result of stress. Hot towels for the nose, antibiotics for the gland infection, and pills for the panic. "It happens," the doctor said, when I asked for an explanation of my terror. I never took the pills he prescribed, but he suggested a single glass of wine every evening and this medicine I gladly swallowed.

I visited a psychiatrist, explaining that I was in some sort of common midlife crisis, too boring for words, and not really worth his time. We chatted about my fears about my marriage, my desperation to keep our family together, and my religious longings. It turned out he was a former Catholic priest. I explained to him that his ex-church had it all backward: "It's not God is Love; it's Love is God. Our talking to each other right here, right now, is God."

He seemed stunned by this, and said nothing for a while, as if this were real news to him (and maybe it was). But I realized I was up to my old cocktail party shtick of solving personal problems for psychiatrists, and I desisted. I had, however, told him everything I knew, and everything I was trying frantically to hang on to.

I approached a kind of stability again, reassured by the two doctors, and by Annie with sweet sexual healing, that caring was not gone from the universe and that I could live through this. But every morning I woke knowing that my sister-in-law and many friends were suffering—"Debbie is dying" was my first thought of the day—and that panic might still knock me out.

My friend Doris Grumbach, who later endured a nightmare of constant pain from shingles, offered this way out: "To turn the intractable pain to some positive use, I decided to try to live with full awareness of its presence, not just try to ignore it."

Alan Watts once counseled: "Become one with your pain."

Similarly, with sudden bravado, I decided to embrace my recurring panic. "Come for me now! I can outpanic you. Horror, horror everywhere. I know. Tell me something I don't already know, dear panic. I can imagine more terror than you can terrify me with! I can outpanic you, panic!"

I have no idea if that approach will help others, but my refusal to attempt any control of the panic, to just let it be, indeed to welcome it laughing, helped to gradually obliterate it without medication.

As the tower took shape, I put one foot in front of the other, moved from nail to nail, remembering my friend Kirby Williams's advice, based on what used to be called a nervous breakdown he suffered as a young man. Almost immobile with anxiety and exhaustion, he managed to visit his wife's family in England for Christmas. "They were so good to each other, so kind. I didn't want to go crazy and leave that. It was really a turning point. I came back."

I recalled again my beautiful friend Frank Stiffel, who survived those years in Treblinka and Auschwitz and emerged with grace and sanity. I wasn't certain I could be nearly as strong and decent as Frank or Kirby. I might very well lose it all again.

But building helped me heal, and I waited for mind and body to do the rest. "Wait!" I wrote in black Magic Marker on a card pushpinned to the tower sheathing. I began to trust my mind and body again. I knew, as if for the first time, the meaning of the Bible verse "Be still, and know that I am God."

Compared to bouts of free-fall panic, my vertigo would be a holiday, I thought.

Then one breezy dawn, I buoyantly shimmied up through my hatch opening and sat on my roof, all the way up there. The peak at last. I was ready to nail on the roof sheathing and start with the tar paper and rolled roofing. Then I looked over the edge at the rocks below.

It hit me. I could not move. "Petrified" is the precise word.

CRAB

The problem with Intuitive Engineering is that you don't know until later if you have intuited correctly. Would my 2" × 4" rafters, on top of the doubled 2" × 4" ridge beam and the 2" × 6" sub-rafters, collapse under me? Would I receive a warning so that I could get down in time, if I could indeed move at all? I listened for creaks, cracks, and groans from the wood and nails beneath me. Sometimes, I had learned from a previous ladder collapse, there is no warning. A fraction of a second and it's gone, like the ancient Civic Tower of Pavia that "just disappeared."

Would this entire structure topple over with the load of one moderately overweight body up here? Was it even now moving beneath me from side to side or was that just an illusion from the shadows of the wind-whipped leaves across the plywood?

"I can't do this," I whispered to myself. "It's way beyond me. I'll have to call Jim." I was certain Jim Adams scampered over roofs in fearless delight.

But I couldn't even turn myself around to get back down that hatch opening. All sense of balance was gone—and the tower was definitely shifting under me. I wasn't even sure anymore where the roof edges were. Bursts of blinding sunlight, the gyrating shadows, and the rushing clouds in the background left me without any sense of boundaries. I could crawl off into space. The result of a fall onto the rocks below would be the same as a drop from the Eiffel Tower. Death was a few feet away, somewhere.

I thought about calling out "Help!" to the woods. Maybe Opie would have the brains to seek aid with a few barks and a tug on a stranger's sleeve like Lassie? Not likely.

Perhaps my new neighbor, the retired policeman, would hear me and be able to get me down. That's what cops did, wasn't it? No, that was firemen.

Well, maybe the Canadian Micmac Indians far off in the western field, raking shriveled blueberries, would glance up and see me waving. But they never took their eyes from the ground.

Then I remembered the panic cure. Welcome the vertigo. Make it part of you. Wait.

So I sat. The northwest wind blew harder, bending the white birches and the beeches around me. The tower swayed, twisted, and, in a new development, vibrated. If I had been feeling lyrical, I might have said it hummed.

In an hour I was reasonably sure the tower wasn't about to collapse or topple suddenly. I was used to the chaotic movement around me. I waited a bit more, and then, carefully, I inched my body around, hanging onto the hatch framing with both hands, and lowered myself through the hatch hole to the first rung of my ladder and then to the second floor.

I was safe. But I had no prospect for a roof.

That night I walked down the dirt road in Deer Isle to ask Jim for help. I discovered him running toward me in the twilight, training for the Portland marathon.

"She wouldn't be swaying on you. Not with that sheathing," Jim offered, running in place.

"Well, maybe it's all in my mind. Dizziness. You want to roof it for me?"

"Better check the foundation," he said, ignoring my plea.

"It's sitting on a block of granite, Jim."

"Sounds to me like the foundation's got to be where the problem is," Jim insisted. "I'll come by and check it, if you want. This weekend."

I thanked him and let him run off.

At first light the next morning, I returned to the tower and crawled around the foundation. All seemed well. The three cemented J-bolts and metal plates were holding fast to the rocks and girders. My scrap shim under the southern girder was still shimming and leveling.

I pondered the joists protruding a foot over each side of the girders, necessary to make up for the narrowness of the big bang boulder. That overhang had seemed like nothing when I installed the joists, a mere foot over the girders' edges. But that had to be the source of the sway.

I bought four pressure-treated ten-foot-long 2 × 6's at A.J.'s lumberyard and nailed them like spider legs to each corner of the tower, four feet of each nailed with 20d's into the existing joists and six feet extending from the tower to cement blocks and shims at the ends. Eventually, I imagined that the tower would be surrounded by a deck on a row of these spider legs, my

198 / BILL HENDERSON

version of the cathedral-stabilizing flying buttresses (low-flying, in my case).

Once again, far less buoyantly, I ascended through my hatch hole. Although the breeze was milder and the shadows and clouds were not twirling about me, it seemed the tower had indeed stopped swaying. Jim had been right. It was the foundation, stupid.

That morning I tested my vertigo inch by inch. I practiced nailing the sheathing close to me. Then I nailed farther out, not daring to leave the vicinity of the hatch. I noticed that if I concentrated on each nail and its proper pounding, I had no time for vertigo. The hammer and the nail became my focus and point of reference. In that simple way, I could be sure of where I was in the air.

I still wasn't sure I could finish this roof, but at least it was possible for me to get back down and not have to cry out for help.

Then I discovered the secret of amateur, semi-sloping roof-building—the crab scuttle. Sitting firmly on my butt, legs always between me and the roof edge, I could scuttle slowly and cautiously across the sheathing and—speaking rationally at least—never be in danger of pitching off. Through the day I scuttled about that roof in my new crab stance, growing bolder and bolder until, by sunset, I had nailed down all the sheathing and the aluminum drip edges, a protection for the last foot of the roof at the eaves — just before the drop off onto the rocks, a place I could not have hoped to reach the day before.

The next morning I rolled out and tacked down the 36"-wide Number 15 tar paper (also called felt or asphalt paper). I started at the downslope edge, crabbing back up to the ridge behind me, overlapping the tar paper as I went. In the same way, I installed my rolled roofing over the tar paper. It was rolled up just like the tar paper but consisted of a much heavier asphalt and grit mixture. I nailed each edge of the rolled roofing with roofing nails into the plywood below, aiming for the rafters but not always making contact. Then I sealed the nail holes and seams with roofing cement, a nasty black gunk that I applied with the old garden trowel and found stuck to me and to all I wore and touched for a long time thereafter.

By the end of the second day, I had a roof that didn't dare leak and vertigo that had slunk away, defeated by the same spirit that controlled the panic. Embrace it. Wait. Be still.

Finally, after all the heavy construction was finished, it seemed safe to install the very breakable windows. There was nothing fancy about this installation. The four large yard-sale windows with the real wood-divided panes were suspended from hinges in the rough openings upstairs, two in the east and two in the west, and closed down with hook-and-eye fasteners. On the sill under them, I nailed a strip of clapboard, slim side out, to direct the rain down and not in.

The two double-paned slider windows from the East Hampton Dumpster were permanently fixed in their rough openings downstairs on top of outward-sloping clapboard. Here, since wood permanently touched wood and was liable to rot, I first covered the clapboard with metal flashing. The windows were fastened with protruding nailheads on each side and later secured with inside and outside trim over their frames.

Last, my big red dump door with the porthole windows was swung on its hinges and hooked shut. No need for a fabulous lock here. Burglary in Down East Maine is as rare as a spring without black flies, and besides, the best insurance against burglars is to own nothing worth burgling. At the Deer Isle cottage I had posted, just inside the door, this poem by Etta May, an Indiana uplands Quaker:

> *If thee needs anything*
> *And cannot find it,*
> *Just come to me*

And I'll tell thee
How to get along
Without it.

In the last days of that summer, I constructed a simple eight-by-eight-foot deck on the roof—two 2" × 4" pressure-treated boards laid flat and nailed into the rafters through the roof at three spots (sealed with roof gunk) and a platform of 1" × 6" × 8' spruce planks hammered across the two boards and over the ridge, touching a strip of metal flashing at the ridge for a third support.

A rustic railing of 4" × 4" × 3½' uprights at the four corners and 2" × 4" × 8' cross rails finished the small deck, which later might become a belfry or whatever—a vision for next summer that I would intuit all winter.

Intoxicated with my vertigo-vanquishing, I left my crab posture. Clinging to my deck railing and holding my breath against fresh surprises, I stood up. I waited for the vertigo to return, for panic, for any new terror that might be thrown at me.

No vertigo. No panic. No new terror.

I took my hands off the railing. I dared to look far out to sea where a vast fog bank was billowing up the coast. I turned again and watched the lights coming on in the hillside town of Stockton Springs on the other side of the Penobscot River.

Then I chanced a look straight up. As I had at the open window of my boyhood bedroom, I reached my hand to the emerging stars and waited for God's touch. Maybe the reaching was that touch.

FOR NO REASON?

After the summer of the "tower for no reason," my mind and spirit, like my smashed fingernails, began a slow recovery using long-stored knowledge.

Once more I began to hear whispers of grace everywhere: in the remembered caring of my dead parents; the love of my wife and child; the everyday kindnesses of strangers that I might have ignored before. As I paced in the drizzle outside a suburban Philadelphia train station after visiting Debbie and Bob, distraught but hopeful that Debbie would miraculously survive her brain cancer (she did), a girl I had never met offered to share her umbrella with me, a tiny gesture that profoundly moved me at that moment.

The whole world is a miracle, said St. Augustine. M. Scott Peck reminds us that "grace and miracles are everyday events. We are just too lazy to see." I might add that many of us are blind because we don't have the time or have lost the imagination to see.

Before returning to Sedgwick in October to prepare the tower for its first winter, I wrote a short prayer that tries to say it all in a few words: "God of love, wonder, and forgiveness, grant me the grace to remember you today and to live my life as a prayer to you. And make me an instrument of your peace."

(Only an instrument. One voice in a world of voices.)

I resolve to kneel and say this prayer every morning. Too often I forget, rushed by some ridiculous errand, too hot and bothered to pause for a few seconds, say my few words, and wait in silence.

I always return to Maine before the start of deer hunting season, before the bullets fly and when the leaves are still at their peak. I do not easily gasp at foliage, but the stunning yellows, oranges, and reds against the bright blues of Maine's ocean and bays usually force more than one sharp intake of breath.

There was finishing work to be done before that first winter roared in and tested what I had constructed.

Inside, I let the sunlight do the decorating. My only contribution was two coats of latex paint for the plywood floors, walls, and ceilings. I used half-price, returned "mistake" paint, pale yellow, dusky white, and pinkish coral. I also supplied a metal double bed with squeaking springs that the label said had been manufactured in 1923 in Utica, New York. With my rope friend, I hauled up the bed, somebody's cast-off kitchen table and chairs in a 1950s mode, plus a cat-scratched, corduroy reclining armchair—all courtesy of the East Hampton dump.

If this were to have been an all-season tower, I would have tacked insulation between the studs and ceiling rafters and nailed Sheetrock or wood paneling over it, and I might have rigged up a woodstove. But I let such possible improvements wait for another year.

For now, I was blessedly free of appliances except for a small Sony portable radio—musical pleasure on long fall nights in the tower. Down East Maine has two terrific all-night classical music stations, plus a virulent transmission from the Christian Right that figuratively burns New Agers and homosexuals at the stake. Such joy they take in crucifying Christ over and over in the name of love.

Outside, I thought more about the third-floor topping. There were many topping styles to consider: the 210-foot Coit Tower in San Francisco is finished off with what is said to be the nozzle of a firehose (though others see salacious pretensions); the now-demolished Dole spire in Honolulu was capped with a giant pineapple (blatant propaganda); Edward Bok's 295-foot Singing Tower in Mountain Lake, Florida, erected to proclaim "the gospel and influence of beauty," supports fifty-seven bronze bells at its peak; a statue of the legendary Jack the Treacle-Eater dances atop a tower in Barwick, England.

For now I opted to stay with my simple and plain deck.

In picking siding to install over my sheathing I had many options: board and batten (Number 3 pine boards nailed into the sheathing with the spaces between boards covered by strips called battens) would enhance the tower with vertical lines, but it was too expensive; cedar shingles were also pricey and very boring to install, shingle by shingle into November perhaps; clapboard seemed a fine New England tradi-tional siding—not the high-priced cedar variety but Number 3 knotty-pine clapboard.

Before nailing on the clapboard with 6d nails that penetrated the sheathing into the studs, I swaddled all four sides with tacked-on tar paper. I prefer the old-fashioned tar paper to the new, more expensive "housewraps" that are said by their various manufac-turers to "breathe."

Then I trimmed all the corners of the window and door openings with 1" × 4" Number 3 pine, later painted with "Forest Green" enamel.

Finally, beginning at the bottom of each side, I started upward with the clapboard, overlapping each board by an inch and a half, as marked on the previous board. From time to time, I'd step back and eyeball the progression of the clapboards to be sure they weren't on a crooked path. As I moved higher, I discovered that clapboards were easy enough for one man to carry up the ladder and hammer on alone, with lots of upping and downing, measuring and cutting and pounding; an exhilarating task in the cool, golden Maine autumn.

For now, I left the clapboards their natural color, treat-ing them only with a coat of clear waterproofing. (Later, when the wood darkened and grew patched with mildew,

I sealed the knots with sealer and stained the tower in a shade dubbed "Cape Cod Gray" by the maker.)

Just before the first gunshot of deer season, I finished treating the clapboards and headed south to Annie and Holly. Further chores and any more progress into the sky would wait for spring.

Through the winter, I pondered from time to time what I had done. Was it really a tower for no reason?

At the start it certainly was. At least I thought so. For sure I could cite a whole host of literary influences from my college days, academic baggage I had been trying to ignore. Lucretius said, "There is nothing more pleasant than to inhabit lofty and serene sanctuaries"; Montaigne wrote his essays in a tower overlooking his garden ("la domination pure"); Milton's "Il Penseroso" celebrated a thinker in his spire pondering mystical doctrine; Shelley's poem "Prince Athanase" immortalized a wise prince in a lonely tower; Rilke inhabited a tower in Switzerland in the early 1920s, bought for him by his patron, and wrote much about towers, too; so did Hart Crane.

But I wasn't aware of any of these influences when I first had a vision of my tower. Only after I had written the first draft of this essay did I actually behold that

Jack the Treacle Eater [*Lauren Jarrett*]

vision in an 1879 etching, *The Lonely Tower* by Samuel Palmer. It's all there, the small tower, the hill, just as I imagined it that morning on Christy Hill with Doris after church services. I do not remember ever seeing that etching before. It's astonishingly accurate. Even the rocky soil is genuine Down East.

Certainly the tower *became* an ersatz church steeple pointing to a God I couldn't find in "organized religion" (a superb oxymoron).

Obviously the tower *became* an escape from a wobbly period in our marriage. Until Annie lured me back with lunch in the woods and other afternoon delights, I seemed determined to become a lone-wolf Thoreau. By the way, Thoreau never married. His first love jilted him and that was it for him and the ladies. If he had married, you can bet we wouldn't have *Walden* to worship. His wife would have had none of that shack. I mean a chair for solitude, one for friends, and another for society. Come on.

Finally, my tower *became* an escape from my sorrow about Debbie's, Kim's, and my other friends' cancers, and my own middle-age hypochondria and panic.

The Lonely Tower, by Samuel Palmer, 1879
[*The Art Museum, Princeton University. Gift of Frank Jewett Mather, Jr.*]

If I were a critical whizbang I could deconstruct this tower of mine down to its first shovel of hardscrabble. And that's what I'd be left with. Dirt.

If you are thinking of constructing your own tower, I suggest that you don't become overly analytical. Resist your shrink's advice that you devote more time and money to psychological explanations for your urges; avoid your doctor's offers of Prozac or Viagra; harden your heart against your spouse's complaint that what you really need is a new washer/dryer combo or a used Volvo.

Every real tower is impractical. As I have said for our purposes, all other towers are mere utilitarian erections. And your tower vision need not be sharply defined, even though your zoning board thinks otherwise. Maybe you want to make it up as you go along. Maybe what you are dreaming of is just a place to go and dream. Put that in language a bureaucrat can understand, and proceed. And by the way, you don't need a hill in Maine to raise your tower on either. Your backyard will do fine, as Sam Rodia showed us.

If you are thinking of trying a tower, perhaps the following economies (with thanks to Thoreau's original *Walden* expense sheet) will be helpful. I compiled my list that first winter as the black bears slept and the Maine snows swirled. Some prices were rounded off or estimated if copies of bills were lacking. (Maine sales tax not included.)

EXPENSES

Gloves (garden gloves from the supermarket) . . . . $ 1.99

Hammer. . . . . $ 14.00

Saw . . . . $ 9.98

Tri-Square. . . . . $ 10.00

Level. . . . . $ 9.80

Rope (50 feet, ⅜") . . . . $ 12.60

Ladder . . . . borrowed

Joist hangers (12 @ $1.95) . . . . $ 23.40

Nails: 20d (5 lbs. @ 80¢) . . . . $ 4.00

        16d (20 lbs. @ 80¢) . . . . $ 16.00

         8d (10 lbs. @ 75¢) . . . . $ 7.50

         6d (8 lbs. @ 75¢) . . . . $ 6.00

Foundation. . . . .   free

Cement (one bag) . . . . $ 5.58

Rebar (various lengths). . . . . $ 6.60

Metal anchor plates (3 @ $9.00) . . . . $ 27.00

Pressure-treated girders (2, 6" × 6" × 12' @ $22.50). . . . $ 45.00

Pressure-treated joists (18, 2" × 6" × 10' @ $6.80) . . . . . $ 122.40

Untreated joists for low-flying buttresses

   (12, 2" × 6" × 10' @ $4.90) . . . . $ 58.80

Second-floor joists (7, 2" × 6" × 10' @ $4.90). . . . . $ 34.30

First-floor wall studs (26, 2" × 4" × 8' @ $2.40) . . . . $ 62.40

Second-floor wall studs (26, 2" × 4" × 7' @ $1.90). . . . . $ 49.40

Sills and plates (24, 2" × 4" × 12' @ $3.90). . . . . $ 93.60

Plywood (33, 4' × 8' ½-inch CDX @ $13.90) . . . . $ 458.70

Window and door trim (120 feet, 1" × 4" No. 3 pine) . . $ 175.00

Planks for low-flying buttress deck,

    balcony and dream deck

    (46, 1" × 6" × 12' @ $5.50) . . . . $ 253.00

Tar paper (three rolls @ $15.50). . . . . $ 46.50

Drip edge strips (two) . . . . $ 21.00

Rolled roofing (one roll) . . . . $ 34.98

Roofing cement (one can) . . . . $ 5.95

Clapboard (assorted lengths, 2" × 6", No. 3 pine) . . . . . $ 398.00

Clear waterproofing (2 gals. @ $21.00) . . . . $ 42.00

"Mistake" paint (4 gals. @ $9.96). . . . . $ 39.84

Paint brushes (3 disposable 3½" @ $2.95). . . . . $ 8.85

Large first-floor windows (two) . . . .   free

Small first-floor window (one) . . . .   free

Large second-floor windows (4 @ $10.00) . . . . $ 40.00

Hatch cover (small Plexiglas storm window) . . . .   free

Entrance door (one). . . . .   free

Balcony door (one). . . . .   free

Various furnishings. . . . .   free

Hinges and hooks. . . . . $ 20.39

Other stuff . . . . $ 100.00

Total $2,264.56

(Not included in this total is the cost of sealer and stain and various minor improvements the following year. Also omitted is the $50 for the hired backhoe and various bags of cement, rebar, and hardware for that failed first attempt, which is now blessedly being covered over by brush and brambles.)

I could have saved money if I had hand-chopped trees and sawn the wood for studs, joists, rafters, sheathing, siding, and planks. In fact, my economies might have compared with Thoreau's. But I had to get my tower under cover before winter undid my work. And while I may brag that I saved cash by doing without power tools, it was only I that did without the power. The lumberyard delivered wood in a gas-slurping truck; an anonymous mill somewhere fashioned all of my lumber with gigantic machines that I would have found appalling had I dropped in for a visit.

Like Thoreau, who used a borrowed ax made in a factory somewhere near Concord, I did the best I could with "my economies." And putting together that modest tower was a priceless rediscovery of my spirit. Through the inspiration and courage of my daughter, my wife, my family and friends, I learned to know again what I already knew: love the Lord your God with all your heart, soul, and mind, and love your neighbor as you love yourself. That's what it's all about, like he said. (And so tough to remember.) Nothing else much matters, including all the towers of the earth.

Christy Hill tower in winter [*Bill Henderson*]